GETTING TEAMWORK RIGHT

The key to happy, successful and resilient teams

ANDY FIELDHOUSE

RETHINK PRESS

First published in Great Britain in 2020
by Rethink Press (www.rethinkpress.com)

© Copyright Andy Fieldhouse

For Tanya, Matilda and Oliver

Contents

Introduction

How many people are alive in the world right now? As I write this, we are over the seven billion mark. I remember reading the paper when the number ticked over five billion. Why is this relevant? I mention it for two reasons.

First, within this global population, there must be a huge number of teams out there trying to get things done. And second, this incredible population growth is putting pressure on our world like never before, and the only way we will be able to overcome these pressures is by working together in teams.

Why I wrote this book

I became a parent for the first time in 2014. Any parent will tell you that it is a life-changing experience. You are suddenly responsible for a new, tiny and perfect human being. I have two children now and I feel the strong protective instincts towards both of them that all parents feel. You desperately want them to be safe and happy and you want to provide them with the best possible start in life.

I found myself thinking about the world that my wife and I have brought them into. What sort of a world will it be when they are adults? What sort of a world will it be when I am gone? What will it be like for my grandchildren? You would be forgiven for thinking it could be a bit of a mess on current evidence. I'll admit to feelings of fear and worry for my children's future. Their world could be a difficult place to be, and I feel the urge to do what I can to help prevent them from having to struggle and fight for a happy existence, or even for survival.

I firmly believe that if human beings are going to have any chance of making it through the next 100 years, they need to be able to work together in teams. Also, fixing what's broken, solving some of the global challenges facing humanity and preventing further damage to the fabric of our existence is not going to be the preserve of scientists and politicians – it is going to be up to all of us to be better at working together. Collaboration, communication, leadership, self-sacrifice, empathy and social intelligence are going to be key to helping the human race survive and thrive long into the twenty-first century and beyond.

So, what could I do to help make this earth a better place for my kids to grow up and live in?

I have spent many years helping teams to work more effectively together. I have witnessed all that is good and bad about how teams work, what they get right, and what they get wrong. I have researched the topic of teamwork, written and spoken about it, trained, taught and coached the skills of teamwork to hundreds of teams made up of people from all over the world.

In that time, I have worked out the key behaviours and practices necessary for any team to succeed and enjoy the experience along the way.

My answer to a better future has been to put all my knowledge and experience about how to get teamwork right into this book, for you to benefit from the lessons I have learnt throughout my career to date. I can't change the world overnight, but every journey starts with a single step, and I can start with this book.

What is in this book?

This book contains what I believe you need to do to have a happy and successful team – whether that's your work team, family or sports team. I have written it to achieve two things. First, to raise awareness of the essential aspects of teamwork that you need to work on, why they are important and why you need to do something about them. Second, I offer advice on what you can do to improve these aspects of your team's life.

I have presented these aspects as topics to answer some of the core questions around teamwork, including:

- What is your team's purpose and why it is important to identify that and connect people to it?

- Who should be on a team?

- How can a team ensure it succeeds?

- How should the team communicate?

- How should the team handle leadership?

- What culture or atmosphere should the team have?

No team is perfect – some are decidedly imperfect. We are human, after all, and are therefore essentially flawed. And we bring our faults and foibles to the way in which we interact and work with other humans in the teams we are part of, whether that's at work, at home or at play.

I am astounded sometimes by the inability of teams to work successfully together. Maybe I shouldn't be. After all, when are we ever taught teamwork skills? Education is changing, but there are still plenty of us who were taught geometry, and who won the Battle of Hastings, but were never taught how to be empathetic, how to communicate, or how to control our emotional selves. I cover these and many other teamwork skills in this book.

Who is this book for?

This book is essentially for anyone who exists in a team – which is nearly all of us – and who wants to learn how to improve the way that team interacts and works together. It's not just for team leaders, it's for anyone on the team, and I have written it in an approachable, accessible style to ensure you can take away some real and actionable measures to help your team.

Getting teamwork right sometimes takes courage, effort and sacrifice. But the rewards are worth it. There's a magic that happens when teams click and start to really function. And if I can move the needle in the right direction for a few people and teams by writing this book, maybe it will help to sow some small seeds for a brighter and better future for the world, and for my children.

ONE
The Teamwork Paradox

The human race is at a crossroads. We face an uncertain future. I don't need to tell you that. It's everywhere you turn. Politically, economically, socially, geographically, linguistically, at work, at home, at play – no stone has been left unturned by the forces of radical and exponential change. And the pace of this change is only getting faster.

One thing though remains the same. At a basic level, we as a species work together to get nearly everything done. Since our ancestors first started hunting in packs hundreds of thousands of years ago, teamwork has been an intrinsic part of the human condition and experience. Humans have honed their teamwork skills over millennia, passed on their aptitudes for collaboration in their DNA and taught their techniques to the generations that followed them.

For many millennia, this rudimentary teamwork was effective. For much of human history, the field of play and the rules in which we worked didn't change much. What you inherited and were taught by your predecessors equipped you to make sure you were fed and defended against attack. And our deepest animalistic instincts, which still subconsciously drive us today, are based upon the requirement to meet those basic human needs.

Fast forward to today's living and working environment and you can reflect upon how much has changed about how we operate as a species. The environment in which we work together as teams is entirely different and, thanks to digital technologies, is still changing – fast. The rules, the opportunities, the very ways in which teams work are unrecognisable to those of our early ancestors. And yet, as a species, humans are failing to evolve at the same pace as the rapid changes in our environment. Despite all the amazing opportunities we have as a result of innovation and the ability to connect and communicate, paradoxically, as teams we are, if anything, going backwards.

Let's assume that around 5,000 years ago marks the point at which we moved into the era of modern civilisation. The modern period has brought a very different way of working in teams compared to the tribes and groups of our earliest incarnations, yet represents a mere 0.08% of our time on the planet. Now consider that the radical changes currently impacting our working in teams, such as global travel, or the advent of the Internet, have only arrived in the last twenty to fifty years – or 0.0003% to 0.0008% of our time since we diverged from apes. In this context, it is easy to appreciate the depth to which we are hardwired in our core DNA to work in teams in a certain, primitive way. A lot of that hardwiring is still valid, but an increasing amount is out of step with the environment in which we now live and work.

Why is teamwork so important, and why should I care?

OK, I get it. You might be thinking this is all very well, but why should I care? This doesn't matter for me, does it? Think again.

Teams are everywhere. They are the vehicles we use to get things done. They are your family, your work team, your football team – even your friendships require teamwork to be fulfilling and meaningful. Teamwork weaves in and out of all parts of our lives, right up to the society, country and planet where we live. Your teamwork skills are intrinsic to every interaction you have with other people in one way or another. This might be in obvious places, like your work team, or it might be more subtle, like the relationship you have with your child or the choir you sing in.

As if this wasn't enough of an explanation as to why you should care about teamwork and its associated skills, and how you could be improving them, then consider this. The very nature of our existence and how we are living and working together in the world is changing beyond measure. I firmly believe that we are going to face a more complicated, uncertain and threatening future, which will require a different level of teamwork and set of skills than we have ever experienced in our long and complicated human history, if we are to survive on this planet.

I don't think I am being overly dramatic by saying this. Some scientists give us a 50-50 chance of making it through the next 100 years – if not in terms of whether we will be extinct as a species, then at least in whether we will still exist in the same numbers and social civilisations we do today. The challenges we face are numerous: climate change, a global population crisis, the increase in drug-resistant viruses, the pressures we are placing on agriculture, fresh water and energy consumption. There's a potentially lethal cocktail of things that we may need to address as a species in the next 100 years, and part of our response to that will involve working together in teams.

When the world fell into the grip of the COVID-19 coronavirus pandemic, governments, countries and

communities had to rapidly adapt and find completely new strategies and ways of collaborating in
order to overcome the virus. The pandemic provides
a perfect example of how global teamwork, including economic and state co-operation and scientific
and medical collaboration, is vital in tackling unprec-
edented challenges affecting the world's population.

Do you still think this is not your problem? I get that.
Maybe I am particularly attuned to my responsibility to society and the future. Becoming a parent six
years ago has made me think more deeply about the
world my children will live in – and I do believe in
the saying that we are only renting this earth from our
children. If you are a parent, one thing you can do for
your children is to learn how to be better at teamwork
for their sake.

Not a parent? Not bothered about the future of the
human race? I can respect that. That's your preroga-
tive, your choice. But what if I tell you that how you
work in any team in the next ten to twenty years is
going to be radically different from now, and if you
don't learn, adapt and change with the times, you will
be left dead in the water. What then?

The pace of change

At the heart of this change in how we live and work
together, which is creating so many opportunities as

well as hindrances, is technology. The Internet has spawned a social media revolution and put information into the hands of the masses through smartphones. A farmer in Africa with a smartphone can access more information than Bill Clinton could when he was President of the United States of America. Your phone may soon be able to diagnose if you are sick or not. We are on the verge of a clean energy boom, driverless cars will be with us within a few years, and we've made robots that can think better than we can. Some people even theorise that the first human to live to 200 has already been born, and our grandchildren will be sitting around in the future saying, 'Can you imagine that our grandparents had to live with only one body?' This kind of stuff is no longer the preserve of science fiction. It is fast becoming fact.[1]

Collaboration and teamwork are the skills around which we will increasingly lead our lives. An article in the January/February 2016 issue of *Harvard Business Review* explains how collaboration is transforming the workplace:

> 'As business becomes increasingly global and
> cross-functional, silos are breaking down,
> connectivity is increasing, and teamwork
> is seen as a key to organizational success.

---

1   David Goldhill, 'There is someone alive today who will live to 1000
     years old: Why are we living longer than ever?', *The Independent*,
     2018, www.independent.co.uk/news/long_reads/live-longer-
     longevity-stem-cells-ageing-a8332701.html, accessed 23 March 2020.

According to data we have collected over the past two decades, the time spent by managers and employees in collaborative activities has ballooned by 50% or more'.[2]

Evidence from the world of work is also mounting as to not only how important teamwork is, but how different it is becoming. General Stanley McChrystal wrote a *New York Times* best seller in 2015 called *Team of Teams*, which tells the story of how he restructured the US Special Forces to combat a completely different enemy in Iraq and Afghanistan. He took them from a clunky, slow twentieth-century model to a fluid and agile twenty-first century organism that was able to succeed in this ever-changing modern environment. He says of their experience:

'Our transformation is reflective of the new generation of mental modes we must adopt in order to make sense of the twenty-first century. If we do manage to embrace this change, we can unlock tremendous potential for human progress.'[3]

In the 2017 Deloitte Global Human Capital Survey, which collated results from more than 10,000 human resources practitioners and leaders in over

---

2 Rob Cross, Reb Rebele and Adam Grant, 'Collaborative overload', *Harvard Business Review*, 2016, https://hbr.org/2016/01/collaborative-overload, accessed 28 February 2020.
3 Stanley McChrystal, Tantum Collins, David Silverman and Chris Fussell, *Team Of Teams*, p251.

140 countries, the accelerating rate of change and its impact were clear:

> 'Organizations face a radically shifting context for the workforce, the workplace, and the world of work. These shifts have changed the rules for nearly every organizational people practice, from learning to management to the definition of work itself.'[4]

What does this all mean?

In summary, I wish to communicate three truths to you:

TRUTH #1: The playing field of life upon which are the teams you are part of is changing, and changing fast. If you and your team don't change with it, you will be left behind.

TRUTH #2: Teamwork is an intrinsic part of life, and it's in your interest to know how to get it right, if you want to be happy and succeed.

TRUTH #3: We are all going to need to work better together if we are to make the best of the opportunities

---

4   Deloitte, '2017 Global Human Capital Trends: Rewriting the rules for the digital age', *Deloitte Development LLC*, 2017, https://documents. deloitte.com/insights/HCTrends2017, p2.

this brave new world presents us with, to thrive – or even survive – in the future.

Don't throw the baby out with the bath water

Let me get something straight. I am not saying that we must change *everything* we do in teams. Far from it. A lot of what we do is absolutely the right thing and still completely valid practice today. We shouldn't be throwing the baby out with the bath water. No, we should be keeping what is good, tweaking it, and adding in some new techniques that are more relevant for what we need today. A lot of what I am going to talk about, we already know about and have done for years. Some of this is therefore affirmation, proof that what we have been doing is still worthwhile. Some of it is also stuff that we *suspected* worked, but which advances in science and technology have enabled us to check, measure and *prove* works, which we couldn't do a few years ago. It's a case of saying what is best, what is not, and what is new that you can add on to what you might already be doing.

The teamwork paradox

The paradoxical situation we face is this: we have created fantastic tools and ways in which we can work together, and yet we seem to be getting worse at it.

Individuals are hiding behind their public, social media persona, and countries are becoming more protectionist and less open. We are not making the most of the opportunities presented to us to collaborate and work together more effectively, at either a macro or micro level.

Many teams are still not getting teamwork right. Sadly, all too often I see teams that have some dysfunctional behaviour going on. Conflict, confusion, low morale, ineffective or even destructive communication, working in silos – these and a long list of other faults are evident in so many teams, large and small.

It's time to make the best of the incredible opportunities that technological innovation and a greater understanding of human development are giving us. It's time to get teamwork right and unleash the true potential within your team to ensure you have a happier and more successful existence.

TWO

Purpose

Teams exist for a reason

Teams exist for a reason. Identifying that there is a need to bring people together to do something is the birthplace of a team. At its core is a belief that something needs to be done. A team is not a group of people who gather, for example, to look at a piece of art in a gallery in silence, then walk away. Nothing has been achieved there. Nothing has been shared. Individuals have just existed in the same place at the same time, to get something out of the experience for themselves.

Jon Katzenbach and Douglas Smith define a team as 'a small number of people with complementary skills, who are committed to a common purpose, set of performance goals and approach for which they hold themselves mutually accountable.'[5] A team comes together to do something, to achieve something, to change something.

There's something scientific in that force must be applied to move something from A to B. A metaphorical lever must be pulled, dials turned, buttons pressed. Actions must happen. Change must take place, and it has to be a group of people working interdependently towards this change for the term 'team' to apply to them.

The reason can be big or small, complex or simple, take longer than a lifetime to complete or be finished in minutes. It doesn't matter – all that matters is that there is a reason and that the members of that team are working in harmony to that end.

For a successful team, it is important that the following conditions exist:

- The team has a reason

- The reason includes a compelling purpose and goals for fulfilling that purpose

- The purpose and goals are clearly communicated and understood by everyone on the team

---

5   Jon R Katzenbach and Douglas K Smith, 'The discipline of teams', in *HBR's Top 10 Must Reads – On Teams*, p39.

- The reason inspires discretionary and interdependent effort from the team members

- The team can measure and see progress towards the completion of the goals

The team must have a reason

This may sound obvious, but you would be surprised how many teams can't say what their reason is or take too long to do so. It should be something that every team member can clearly articulate without hesitation. Sometimes there are too many reasons or they just aren't clear enough, or even contradict each other.

As time goes by, teams can get bogged down by the repetitive minutiae of their day-to-day existence and the daily grind overwhelms them. It can be soul-destroying to be working hard but not know where you are going. Imagine climbing a mountain where you don't know how high it is, or how long it will take. You find yourself getting excited because you feel yourself getting towards the top, only to find what you thought was the pinnacle is a false summit and another slope rises up to meet you. How many more of these are there? You don't know. How far are we from the top, or the bottom, for that matter? Don't know. What exactly are we doing here? Don't know.

You and your team members have got to be clear on the basic reason for your team's existence, and make sure you remain focused on that.

The difference between purpose and goals

Margaret Heffernan, international businesswoman and an adviser to CEOs, author and TED Speaker, has spoken eloquently about identifying the driving goals of companies. When she learns that a company has set financial goals, such as achieving 60 billion dollars revenue, her response is revealing:

> 'What on earth makes you think that everybody is going to give it their all to hit a revenue target? You know you have to talk to something much deeper inside people than that.'[6]

Heffernan talks about the need to really connect people with a purpose that makes a difference in their lives every day, so that they willingly do the best work that they can.

There is a distinction between goals and purpose, a difference between the head and the heart. The head looks at the goals of the team. The heart is concerned with its purpose. Goals are the measure of what you are doing, purpose is the deeper emotional driver of why

---

6   TED Radio Hour, 'The meaning of work', 2015, www.npr.org/programs/ted-radio-hour/443411154/the-meaning-of-work, accessed 28 February 2020.

you are doing it. You need to ensure that everyone on your team is clear on both the purpose and meaning behind what they are doing and the measurable goals that will indicate whether they are succeeding and delivering against that purpose and reason for being.

Purpose

On 12 September 1962, President John F Kennedy stood on the podium in Rice University football stadium. It was hot. Thirty-five thousand people sat perspiring under the sun waiting to hear their president give what has turned out to be one of the most iconic speeches of the twentieth century. Kennedy spoke of great achievements conquered, such as flying over the Atlantic and climbing the world's highest mountain, and one achievement yet to be realised – the first moon landing:

> 'We choose to go to the moon in this decade
> and do the other things, not because they are
> easy, but because they are hard, because that
> purpose will serve to organize and measure
> the best of our energies and skills, because that
> challenge is one that we are willing to accept,
> one we are unwilling to postpone, and one
> which we intend to win.'[7]

---

7   NASA Video, 'President Kennedy's speech at Rice University', 2013, www.youtube.com/watch?v=WZyRbnpGyzQ, accessed 28 February 2020.

The race was on. NASA was tasked with putting a man on the moon within the decade, before the Soviet Union had managed to do it. A couple of years into this massive undertaking, a journalist visited NASA and came across a cleaner mopping the floors. He asked what he did at NASA, and the response he received was, 'I am putting a man on the moon.'

I love this story for a couple of reasons. First, the compelling purpose, clearly communicated by the leader, John F Kennedy. It's simple, powerful, inspirational, and not easy to forget. Second, the fact that it resonated with everyone, right down to who some would call the least significant person on the team – the guy who washed the floors. But he was obviously engaged with that purpose, and therefore gave his every effort towards it.

Purpose is such an integral part of teamwork. It's the beginning. The reason for being. And how you create, articulate and live that purpose every day is crucial to your team's success.

'Why are we here?' is the ultimate question to apply to your team. The answer to this is your purpose. Why are you here, what are you here to do, what is the change that you are going to make?

One of the big differences between great teams and the rest is that a great team elicits extra discretionary effort from its members. True greatness requires a fully engaged team of people making the choice to give more and do more than is asked of them.

Why do they do this? Sometimes it's down to their own make-up as a person, which compels them to achieve what is asked of them. Some of the best people I have worked with I class as 'best' because they were like a dog with a bone, they wouldn't let go and if you asked them to do something, they were on it straight away. You are lucky if you have some of these people in your team.

But a lot of people will need to be engaged and motivated to make that choice to do more. Teams packed with people who are just punching a ticket and doing the basics to take home a pay cheque at the end of the week are not going to be the highest performing teams in their field. I did some work once with people who were airline cabin crew, and one of them described this mentality of just doing the basics as the 'chicken or fish approach' – simply going down the aisle dishing out chicken or fish, and that's all they saw their job as. That person didn't get the higher purpose of making their passengers' journey a pleasurable or even exceptional experience.

Most of us need help to make that decision to do more. We need to be inspired, to feel emotionally connected to something bigger than ourselves, to be part of a team that is making a positive impact, creating change for the better and fulfilling our desires. A team needs a compelling purpose to generate this kind of response in its members.

Purpose in the modern world

In the production line- and silo-driven twentieth century, most companies were focused primarily on efficiency and the bottom line. There had been a massive shift at the end of the nineteenth century towards efficiency, led by people like Frederick Winslow Taylor, arguably the world's first management consultant, and Henry Ford, who built and sold the first mass-produced vehicle, the Model T Ford. But efficiency meant workers being told precisely to do a small number of things: 'Sit here and put this wheel on this car. That's all you need to do. Nothing else. Same thing every day. Don't think, just do. For the next forty years until you retire.'

Why you were putting the wheel on that car didn't matter. You just did what you were told. Turned up to work, did your job and went home. There was a total disconnect from the real purpose of the Ford motor company, and how their vehicles improved people's lives. And some would say you didn't need to know that. All you needed to know was how to put as many wheels on cars in your shift as possible.

Fast forward to today's knowledge-driven economy and twenty-first century ways of working. We've seen a sea change in how we work together, with a workforce made up of people increasingly motivated by meaning and impact, who want to know that what they are doing has purpose. Even if they are still in a production line or are a small cog in a big wheel, purpose is important to them. Everyone wants to know that what they are doing, no matter how insignificant it may seem, has some sort of meaning.

Google recently conducted the internal study Project Aristotle to try to uncover what makes a Google team effective. Contrary to their assumptions, 'who is on the team matters less than how the team members interact, structure their work, and view their contributions.'[8] Two of the five key dynamics they identified were meaning of work – 'Are we working on something that is personally important to us?' – and impact of work – 'Do we fundamentally believe that the work we are doing matters?'

In my experience, these two key dynamics are true for most workers today, which is why working on purpose is an absolute must for any team that has the ambition to be successful.

---

8   Julia Rozovsky, 'The five keys to a successful Google team', *re:Work*, 2015, https://rework.withgoogle.com/blog/five-keys-to-a-successful-google-team, accessed 28 February 2020.

What should my team's purpose be?

I can't of course actually answer this question for you. But I can help you work it out.

It's important that you think about two key factors when creating your team's purpose:

1. What is the impact of our actions on the lives of other people?

2. What is the positive effect our actions are going to have on those people?

These are what really motivate us. Unless you are an out-and-out psychopath, you will care about other people and feel good if you can make them feel better. If you can create a clear message to your team that the work they are doing will have a positive impact on other people, you are on your way to creating inspirational, meaningful purpose.

Adam Leipzig gives a great TED Talk on how to find your life purpose in five minutes. He says you need to ask five questions: 'Who you are, what you do, who you do it for, what those people want and need, and how they change as a result.'[9] These are great questions to ask about your team. The answers will anchor

---

9   Adam Leipzig, 'How to know your life purpose in 5 minutes', *TEDx Talks*, 2013, www.youtube.com/watch?v=vVsXO9brK7M, accessed 28 February 2020.

what you do and clearly identify the people you serve and the positive impact you make in their lives.

For some teams and jobs this is going to be easier than others. Doctors, farmers and teachers should find this pretty easy. They work directly to meet the basic human needs of health, food and education. Investment banks, oil companies and engineers might find it harder to define how they meet people's needs, but they do. You will be surprised. If you can make that link between what your people are doing day in, day out, and how it is having a positive effect on other people's lives, then you are going to have a better chance of attaining the goals that need to be reached along the way.

Is purpose the responsibility of the leader or the team?

If you now agree that purpose is important and you need to find it and articulate it, who should do so? Is it only the job of the team leader? I don't think so. Yes, the leader is ultimately responsible for the success or failure of the team, so they have a vested interest compared to their team members, and therefore will be instrumental in instigating purpose and communicating it. But it would be more engaging and get more buy-in if everyone on the team has the opportunity to be part of the discovery process. It's far more powerful to involve everyone and give them an opportunity to have input, share their opinion and listen to others' ideas than to just introduce the purpose, fully formed, to the team.

You also don't have to wait for the leader to find purpose. You can work it out yourself.

A study was done in a hospital in America on how the cleaning staff viewed their jobs. Scientists interviewed twenty-eight cleaners and asked them about the nature of their work. They found that the cleaners could be divided into two distinct groups.

On one hand, people viewed their jobs as mundane and uninspiring, so they basically did the minimum necessary to meet the performance requirement. They turned up, did the work and went home without much further thought.

The second group, however, saw things completely differently. They understood that their work had a direct impact on the wellbeing of patients and their families and were therefore motivated to voluntarily do more than was asked. This second group of cleaners:

> '…altered the task and relational boundaries
> of the job to include additional work tasks,
> as well as frequent interactions with patients,
> visitors, and others in their unit. Members of
> this group liked the job, enjoyed cleaning, felt
> the work was highly skilled, and engaged in
> many tasks that helped patients and visitors

and made others' jobs in the unit (e.g., nurses, clerks) go more smoothly.'[10]

These people were doing the same job, but some of them just chose to look at it differently. Nothing other than their personal attitude was different. People in the second group were doing things like checking the ceilings in patients' rooms were clean – this task was not on the job description but they did it because they worked out that the patient's view for most of the day was the ceiling. One cleaner working on the floor with patients in comas changed the pictures between rooms periodically, because she felt it might help their recovery if their environment was refreshed.

The most striking thing was their response to the question, 'What do you do here?' Cleaners in the first group responded with 'I am a cleaner', or words to that effect. In the second group, one person said, 'I am an ambassador for the hospital'. One respondent even said, 'I am a healer', because she saw her job as keeping the rooms sterile so the patients could heal better or quicker.

Who is most likely to give more, do more, be more engaged and increase the performance ability of the whole team, ie the hospital? Of course, the people in group two. The cleaner who sees themselves as a

---

10   Amy Wrzesniewski and Jane Dutton, 'Crafting a job', *Academy of Management Review*, 2001, p191.

healer is absolutely nailed to the overall purpose of the team – to heal patients.

You don't have to wait for someone else to tell you what your and your team's purpose is. If you can do it all together, that is better, but you are the master of your own destiny in so many ways. As long as you are working within the guidelines set by your job role and the values and culture of the team and organisation you work for, there's no reason you can't figure out what your team's purpose is, and therefore what your reason for being in that team and doing the work is, too.

A 'how to' guide for purpose

This section looks at some things you can do to uncover and develop your team's purpose and connect to it.

Identify who you serve and the impact you make

I've already said that we as human beings are highly motivated by doing things that positively impact other people. The first thing you should do when deciding your team's purpose is to identify the people you serve. This might not necessarily be the customer your company sells to. If you are in a finance function, for example, you might serve more people within the company than outside it. Who are these people? How do you serve them? What positive impact do you make on their daily life? The more emotive the connection, the better.

Hold a discovery session

Get the team together to have an open session on discovering your purpose. Give everyone a voice and listen to their thoughts and opinions. The ground rules for this session should be:

- Everyone on the team attends if possible. If they can't, they should give their thoughts beforehand to a colleague who can share them in the session.

- Pitch the meeting as an open creative session. No idea is too stupid, and anything can be said (within the realms of common decency, of course).

- Everyone should have the chance to speak and should be heard. You may need someone to chair the meeting and manage the discussion to make sure that no one dominates the conversation.

Ask the people you serve what they think

Once you have identified the people you serve, you could involve them by asking what they think, if appropriate (for example, you may be more likely to ask a trusted business partner rather than, say, a prospective customer). Their opinion may open your eyes to benefits they experience that you haven't even thought of.

Make sure your purpose is aspirational rather than defensive

An aspirational purpose is one that is driven by a desire to accomplish compelling goals in the service of something that inspires, excites or rewards. It focuses on the benefit to others, or the chance to push boundaries of innovation, exceed existing records or achieve things not done before. A defensive purpose, on the other hand, is one that is preventative and reactive to other factors. It focuses on things like beating the competition, or just keeping pace with innovation in your industry – 'We have to do this, or else' rather than 'We want to do this'. One is positive, the other decidedly negative.[11] Make sure that your team's purpose is aspirational, not defensive. It will be more compelling, engaging and inspiring.

Create an elevator pitch of your purpose

Once you have worked it out, you need to refine how you articulate your purpose. If you aren't already familiar with the concept of an elevator pitch, imagine you get into an elevator with someone else who is going up one or two floors and they turn to you and

---

11 For more on this concept, read Amy Edmondson, *Teaming*, pp100–102.

ask, 'What's your purpose?' You only have the time it takes to ride to their floor to spit it out. You might have a fairly long-winded or complicated purpose at this point. You need to be able to condense it into a sharp, impactful phrase or sentence.

Your 'elevator pitch' may not necessarily be what you would actually say to pitch your company to someone in thirty seconds. But this concept can be used internally to remind your team clearly and succinctly what your purpose is.

Bring your purpose to life

Now you have your elevator pitch nailed, don't lock it away where no one can see it. Bring it to life. If you are the leader, you have to be the CRO – the Chief Reminding Officer. It's your responsibility to make sure everyone is constantly reminded that everything they are doing is working towards fulfilling this purpose. Say it as often as possible, until you are blue in the face and people are fed up of hearing it. Well, almost fed up – I mean to the extent that they are saying 'We know boss, it's…' off the top of their heads, without hesitation. Write it on the walls, use the question, 'What have you done recently to support our purpose?' when having a check-in with your team. Do whatever you think is reasonable to bring it to life.

Don't be afraid to have fun with it

Don't think that your purpose must be serious. It should be emotional and impactful, but you can make it fun. OK, not everyone can do so – surgeons might struggle – but if there's room, do so. You can have fun with how you live it, too.

Celebrate when your team do things that live up to your purpose

When the team demonstrate that they are living up to your purpose, celebrate, recognise and reward them. When people go the extra mile to deliver against the purpose, or a particular individual does something they have previously struggled with that contributes, however small, then make a big deal of it. If as a leader you are going to praise someone, then make sure you do so in front of their peers – we all love it when everyone else sees we are being recognised by the boss for our good work.

Create your team's specific purpose, distinct from that of the whole organisation

If your team is one of many under the umbrella of a larger organisation, your organisation may well already have a purpose alongside its values. I would still advocate that your team generate its own purpose in line with the one set by the whole organisation. It then becomes more specific and personal to your team and the individuals on it.

Work on your own purpose

Like the cleaners in the hospital, if your team hasn't done this yet and won't for whatever reason, don't wait. You owe it to yourself to see your job as rewarding and meaningful. If you can see a real purpose in what you do, you will enjoy your job more and are more likely to benefit from the extra effort you'll put in as a result.

Share stories from the people you serve

I gave a talk in Slovenia once, and one of the guys in the audience came up to me afterwards because he was struggling to motivate his staff. Most of them worked on a production line making the kind of products you find in pharmacies, and they were just going through the motions. Morale was low, and he was struggling to get them to do anything other than the bare minimum necessary to take their pay cheque home at the end of the day.

I asked him if these people knew what the things they were making did. Were they aware of the positive impact they were having on people's lives? I thought there must be so many success stories, life-changing stories, where their products had made a difference.

As the parent of small children, I assured him that these kinds of products make a huge difference to my family. And I am sure that out there, there will be stories of how these products have either saved lives, or significantly improved the quality of life for the people who bought them. He shook his head, and said no, they didn't do anything to connect the workers with the impact the products had beyond the production line.

My advice for him, as it is to you, is to go away and find real instances where all the effort your team goes through has made the difference you were striving for. If people can see their actions are truly delivering, especially if they do not have a direct connection with the people they serve, this will be hugely motivational. What we are trying to do here, after all, is to inspire the team to make that discretionary choice to give more and do more than asked of them. That's the difference between a good team and a great one.

THREE
Goals

Every team has goals. Goals are the things that your team sets out to achieve. They are the reason for the levers you pull, the buttons you press and the changes you make. They are the items you produce or the service you provide. Teams form to do things and goals are a measure of that output.

Don't confuse a goal with purpose. Like I said earlier, your team's purpose is an emotional factor that pulls at the heart strings, that inspires and excites, that creates meaning and desire. Goals are driven by the head. Strategic and analytical, unemotional dots on your journey towards the top of your team's mountain. The goals are the various camps that you must reach on your way to the peak of your Everest. They serve your purpose and allow you to know where you are along that journey and how far you have to go.

Goals are always there for a team and you need to make sure you have defined them and are measuring yourself against them. If you don't, then you have no indication of progress, no sense of accomplishment and no idea when you have attained success. Without this direction, people are going to quickly disengage, and morale will drop. People like to be successful. If we can't measure ourselves against some sort of benchmark, we can quickly lose our way. Imagine getting on a ship with no idea of where it's going or how long it will take. How confused, bored or even scared would you be?

How to work with goals

It's not enough to just come up with a goal and think everything's going to flow from there. There's a right and a wrong way to work with your goals, from choosing them in the first place, to how you monitor your progress against them.

Choose the right goals in the first place

This might sound obvious, but you would be surprised how many teams are chasing irrelevant numbers. Keep challenging any ideas that you come up with as potential goals. Does that measure deliver towards your purpose? Is this number relevant? Can we control it? Don't necessarily think that your measure needs to be a revenue target. Yes, ultimately revenue counts for all businesses, but what's the thing you are doing that makes it happen? Revenue is a result. The more important goal to measure is in the work you are doing that is bringing the revenue in.

After President Kennedy articulated his inspiring and compelling purpose in his 'We choose to go to the moon' speech, he went on to discuss how they were going to get there:

> 'But if I were to say, my fellow citizens, that we shall send to the moon, 240,000 miles away from the control station in Houston, a giant rocket more than 300 feet tall, the length of this football field… and then return it safely to earth, re-entering the atmosphere at speeds of over 25,000 miles per hour, causing heat about half that of the temperature of the sun and do all this, and do it right, and do it first before this decade is out, then we must be bold.'[12]

OK, so neither I nor JFK are going to help you decide your actual goals, but there are some great lessons in what he said – and this relates to the acronym SMART. First coined in 1981,[13] this mnemonic provides a tried

---

12 NASA Video, 'President Kennedy's speech at Rice University'.
13 George Doran, 'There's a S.M.A.R.T. way to write management's goals and objectives', *Management Review*, 1981.

and tested method when it comes to setting goals. I'm all for looking at new ways of doing things, but in the spirit of 'if it isn't broken, don't fix it,' I still think you should consider using SMART, which stands for Specific, Measurable, Achievable, Relevant and Time-bound.

Let's look at JFK's statement with SMART in mind.

- Specific – 'We shall send to the moon'

- Measurable – '240,000 miles away... 300 feet tall... 25,000 miles per hour'

- Achievable – With a 'bold' approach and enough effort, it is possible

- Relevant – Hugely so in the context of the Cold War and the space race against the Soviet Union

- Time-bound – 'Before the decade is out'

If you are working at NASA in the 1960s, it's pretty clear. Get a man to the moon and back safely before 1 January 1970. It's the ultimate SMART objective.

Let's look at an alternative scenario. Imagine we are on a team selling cars, and the boss comes and tells us, 'Just sell cars'. OK, that's a given. But when we start selling cars, how will we know how we're doing? Are we selling the right cars? We have too many questions. There are too many variables. It's too vague. And it's not measurable. If the very essence of teamwork is to achieve your purpose and goals together, you must be able to tell whether or not you are actually doing that.

What the boss should say is, 'Sell 100 Fords in the first quarter'. He's immediately made it SMART. We can measure ourselves against that. We know exactly what the goal is and when it must be completed by.

You can use the acronym SMART to check any goal you set. It's not the newest tool in the box, but it's tried and tested – and it works.

Select goals that everyone can relate to

Revenue is important to every company. But how does the receptionist or the guy driving the van influence revenue? You need to find goals that everyone can relate to and which contribute towards the success of the team. A company I worked for gave the receptionist a goal of counting the number of smiles she managed to put on the faces of visitors to our office. One point for every smile, five points if they laughed out loud. This wasn't encouraging her to be a clown, but we had worked out that the visitor experience to our office was important. Creating a great first impression for a prospective client went a long way towards whether we were likely to win their business, which would contribute to our revenue. The receptionist could totally understand this goal, why it mattered, and what she could do to influence it.

Find different goals for each person to aim for, which relate to their personal contribution as well as your team's and company's overall goals.

KISS

KISS stands for Keep It Simple, Stupid. Don't over-complicate things for the sake of it. I recommend finding up to five key measures for your team that are your core drivers. But don't create more than needed – if there's only one that counts for you, just have that. Don't look for five if these aren't obvious to you. These core drivers will be the ones you will look at frequently.

There's a great story about the coach of the Cambridge University rowing crew. His team's aim was, as ever, to beat the Oxford University boat crew in the crucial University Boat Race. Striving for perfection meant that the rowers and coaching staff were constantly looking for the edge over the competition. What could they do differently, what could they innovate, intro-duce, change or improve? They kept coming up with ideas and running them past the coach.

One of the issues with this brainstorming was focus. All their innovative thinking was leading them down a path that was not productive, side-tracking them away from what really mattered. To keep them mov-ing in the right direction, the coach would always respond to a suggestion with, 'Will it make the boat go faster?' That's it. It was that simple. Because if they made the boat go faster, they would beat the opposition.

It can be helpful to reflect on this question at critical points for your team. If what is being proposed is not aligned to your team's core purpose and will not make your 'boat go faster', discard it and find an alternative goal instead.

Allow enough time – but just enough

One of the measures of a high-performance team is the speed at which they move, and the fact that they achieve things on or ahead of time. But there is little point putting unrealistic deadlines on your team. If you don't allow enough time to do things, you will only be setting your team up for failure, which is unfair and demoralising. On the other hand, give your team too long and it won't allow them to show what they are truly capable of.

You must be a tightrope walker, who treads the fine line between the two. I can't tell you how much time to allow, because that depends on what it is you are trying to achieve. Only you can get a sense of what is realistic and what isn't, what will be a stretch without being impossible, and what is too long. But you must choose a deadline that creates a sense of urgency and need to get to work straight away.

Involve people in the process

You will get far greater buy-in to your goals if you allow the people who are expected to do the work to have some input into the process of deciding what they are. Put yourself in their shoes – how would you feel? How likely are you to make that extra effort if someone comes in and says, 'Here's your goal that we've come up with, now you go off and do it,' versus 'What do you think matters that you contribute and that we can measure you on?' You may find that they are doing crucial things that are greater indicators of success than you had even thought of. You also don't have to accept their ideas – people are more likely to commit if they have at least been heard. If you give them respect by listening and politely explaining why the goal is going to be something different, they are more likely to commit to that goal than if you dictate the goal to them without hearing what they think about it.

Seek commitment from the team

Once you have your awesome, relevant goal that everyone is happy with, you must seek commitment to it from the people who are going to make it happen and hold them accountable. Ask them, 'Will you do what it takes to make this happen?' It's an explicit request, and there's a tremendous power in asking people to respond to it. They have a chance to say no – if they do, you can work on the goal until everyone is happy to say yes. But at some point, the commitment is made. Wherever possible, ask in person. A recent study by Cornell University concluded that people are thirty-four times more likely to agree to a request if it is made face-to-face as opposed to over the phone or by email.[14]

Be serious about the consequences of failure

As part of the process of seeking commitment, strongly emphasise that there is a real expectation that the work gets done, and it's a big problem if it doesn't. Time and time again, I have seen teams generate a lot of excitement and energy when setting goals, quickly followed by a period of lackadaisical atrophy. Within days, their goals have slipped out of mind and out of sight.

If there's no consequence to failure, people won't care. There has to be a real consequence clearly set out from the beginning, one that people don't want to countenance, and that they will work strenuously towards ensuring doesn't happen. But you need to strike the right balance between carrot and stick – incentive and punishment. Don't only have punishment as a tactic – make sure there are plenty of carrots as well to keep your team motivated.

---

14   M Mahdi Roghanizad and Vanessa K Bohns, 'Ask in person: You're less persuasive than you think over email', *Journal of Experimental Social Psychology*, 2017.

As you check on progress, you have every right to seek answers if people haven't done what they said they would do. Don't shy away from uncomfortable questions. But there is a right way and a wrong way to this process, too. Don't pull people up in front of others – praise in public, reprimand in private. Ask why people haven't done what they said they would do, as there might be a perfectly good explanation. If you have framed the goal within the team correctly, and clearly communicated the consequence of failure, there should be a certain cringe factor if they have to admit they have failed, which people really don't want to experience. But they need to feel that responsibility – to the team and the people on it – that they, for whatever reason, haven't moved the needle sufficiently, as they promised they would.

Appoint an owner of each goal

Many people might contribute to the goal, but I advise that you nominate one individual who is responsible for meeting it overall. It's more powerful when seeking accountability that ultimately one person is answerable for the status of that goal. That person doesn't have to be the leader of the team the goal sits with, or even someone who does most of work that makes it happen, but they should be involved in it, so they have an interest. Ideally, that person has volunteered to be the one accountable, as that shows more commitment from the team than having to nominate someone. That individual is more likely to drive things than if you just leave the goal open-ended with no individual held accountable. In that case, everyone can hide behind each other or make assumptions that someone else is responsible, which lessens the chance of your goals being met.

Only check your goals when you have to

You may have a hierarchy of goals split over time. You might have a five-year goal, an annual one, quarterly, weekly, daily. When you review your goals, you don't have to look at all of them, every day. Look at the daily ones daily, weekly ones weekly, and so on. Look at them at the right time and in the right place. If you were looking at goals every day that didn't change because you weren't moving the lever daily, or can't get the data, then don't bother. Just look at what you need to look at, when you need to look at it. Otherwise you are going to confuse and over-complicate matters and waste precious time.

Make goals and progress visible

There's no point coming up with a fabulous goal and then tucking it out of sight for the duration of the time you have set to achieve it. Make it visible to everyone who needs to see it – the people working towards it and the people who need to see the benefit of that work. It doesn't matter where or how you do it, as long as you do. Technology gives us the ability to create wonderful, visual dashboards online, but don't overdo it. A simple whiteboard is often as good as, if not better than, an expensive or complex website. You can put your goals up on walls in the office, have them available on people's smartphones, read them out at meetings, even make them public on your website – do whatever it takes to keep them front of mind.

Have some low-hanging fruit

Which goals should you tackle first? Do you go for the biggest and hardest to complete, or pick off the easy ones straight away? Operational need will dictate to an extent the order in which things happen, but I am personally a believer in getting a score on the board quickly. It's highly motivating to see progress, and if you are spending days or weeks chipping away at something so big that you don't see any completion, you may dent morale. It's far better for the team to see early wins taking place, even if you have deliberately seeded some low-hanging fruit – goals within easy reach that the team can accomplish quickly before moving forwards to the harder ones.

Celebrate success

When you hit goals, celebrate! Success should feel great and be experienced by everyone who has contributed. Don't leave out the receptionist who has collected smile points. Make things fun and enjoyable.

You have to be serious when things aren't happening, so on the flip side you should have fun and enjoy life when you are doing well. This is especially true if you are setting ambitious goals that take a lot of effort to achieve. How you celebrate is up to you, but it's an important thing to do, no matter how small the achievement. There's also a 'Pavlov's dog' behavioural response here; conditioning your team to expect a reward for achieving a goal can motivate them to work towards more and bigger goals in the future – the more fun your team has now, the more effort they'll put in next time.

FOUR

Who

Do you remember being picked for sports teams as a kid? Two children would be appointed team captains and everyone else would line up, waiting to be picked. The captains would take it in turns to pick who would be on their team until no one was left. If you were captain, who would you have picked? The process is a minefield. Yes, you'd have gone for the best players, but what if your brother or sister was in the line-up, would you have picked them? Or your best mate who wasn't any good – would you have picked them before the better player?

The point of mentioning this is that getting the right people on your team is important, but often difficult to get right. Who should be on your team? Obviously, the best people for the job in hand. But who are they?

They're not only people with the right job skills, but also the right team skills to be able to work successfully together to achieve your aims.

The right stuff – CHEERS

What constitutes the right stuff – the attributes, character, mindset and outlook that make up the full house of team skills essential to a perfect team player? Firstly, don't forget, no one is perfect. As much as there is a set of attributes to look for, people are complicated, flawed, emotional beings, and what we are talking about here is not something you can easily measure. What you are looking for are people that display as high a competency as possible, of as many attributes as possible, as often as possible. No one is going to have all these firing at 100%, all the time. We all have off days. We are all decidedly imperfect. But we want people on our team who have at least some, if not all of these going on in their skill set.

The acronym CHEERS will help you remember the six core attributes that make up the anatomy of a great team player. These are:

- Commitment
- Humility
- Empathy
- Ethics

- Respect
- Sacrifice

Commitment

One of the main themes around teamwork is commitment. A commitment is made to form a team to achieve something. A leader is appointed, committed to this cause. Members of the team are chosen, but also those individuals joining the team are committing themselves to be there. The days of slavery, press-gangs and, for most countries, conscription, are behind us. The only team you are part of that you didn't choose is your family, but you can choose to disassociate from them if you decide to. These days, we mostly choose to join teams. We commit to them of our own free will.

A choice, a commitment, is therefore an essential part of the contract an individual makes with their team. And a high level of commitment is a key indicator of a great team player. Team members who are completely committed to the team and what it is trying to do are going to be instrumental in any claims that team makes of greatness.

If you are going to be on a team, you must commit totally to what the team is doing. I see little point in being half-hearted. It won't serve the team, and the team in turn won't serve you. You need to have a great deal of trust and belief in what the team stands for and is doing – so make sure you have that before you do commit. This dovetails with purpose and goals. It is your responsibility when considering whether you join the team to find out what the purpose and goals are. You are not going to commit your full attention and energy to the team if you have any doubt about your belief in its purpose.

When I think of the great people I have worked with on teams, this factor truly stands out. Committed team members contribute so much more than the ones who are only halfway there. They are self-motivated to give more and do more, which in turn generates reciprocity and commitment from others within the team. There is an energy that comes with commitment that means these people get things done. They commit to completing the set goals on time. I have always valued the 'completion mentality' within people I have managed above a lot of things – sometimes it goes a long way to making up for their less desirable characteristics. I'd rather take that fully committed person and some of their baggage over an easier ride with a less committed person.

Humility

Being on a team means that you frequently have to put the needs of the team before your own. Few people realise that professional cycling offers one of the purest examinations of a team that the sporting landscape provides – the Tour de France, the pinnacle that professional cyclists aspire to.

The mental and physical stamina required by the Tour de France has provided a rich history of drama and achievement over many decades. Cyclists punish their bodies for three weeks, covering thousands of kilometres at speeds most of us have difficulty reaching in our cars on our daily commute. It's an epic test of endurance in every sense.

Although there is one cyclist who stands on the podium in Paris clutching the trophy when it's all over, he would not be up there without his teammates. Yet they don't bask in the same limelight that he does. That's not why they do it.

A professional cycling team entering the Tour de France is made up of nine riders, one of whom is their champion, who the team want to put on the podium at the end of the race. That's who all the other cyclists are there for. It's not for their own personal glory at all. The name given to these riders says it all – they are *domestiques*.

A *domestique*'s only purpose is to support and protect the team leader. He will take his turn riding in front of the leader along with the other *domestiques* on the team. He becomes a windbreak, riding into the wind and saving the leader 30% effort, allowing him to conserve his energy for when it matters. The *domestique* drops back to the team car to get food and water and delivers it to his leader. He will even give the leader his bicycle or tyre if the leader's bike breaks or has a puncture, and he will wait for a new one when the team car can get a replacement to him. His personal time means nothing. All his energy is focused on supporting the leader.

The tale of the *domestique* only goes part of the way to describing a humble team player. Humility is the quality of having a modest view of one's importance. The leader who stands on the podium at the end of Le Tour needs to display personal humility. He should be saying things like, 'I wouldn't be here it if wasn't for my team'. The tradition still exists that the winner of the Tour de France voluntarily shares his winnings with his teammates, to say thank you for everything they did to get him there.

Humility happens when you check your ego at the door. Arrogant, egotistical people are poisonous to teams. One of the biggest mistakes made in recruiting people onto teams – and I know, because I have made it – is to fall for someone's skill set, when you know that they are self-centred, arrogant or egotistical, but think it'll be OK because you will be able to handle that side of their character. A lack of personal humility (ie arrogance and ego) is extremely damaging within teams. Even if you think you can manage it, others on the team may not be able to do so. You will find yourself regretting the choice and wishing you'd not chosen this person in the first place.

A word of warning about humility, though. People with low self-esteem are also getting humility wrong, and arguably in a more damaging way than the egotist. It may be well hidden and hard for you or them to recognise and fix. As Pat Lencioni says in his book *The Ideal Team Player*, 'A person who has a disproportionately deflated sense of self-worth often hurts teams by not advocating for their own ideas or by failing to call attention to problems they see.'[15]

Empathy

Empathy is the ability to put yourself in the shoes of other people, to care about how they feel and consider the impact of your actions on their emotions. It's obvious that this is a great trait when you are working with others. It encompasses not only compassion for that person, but a true sense of wanting to help them feel better.

Most of us are, thankfully, empathetic. This is our hardwiring as human animals. We have evolved in tribes and societies to generally care about the people in our immediate circle, so it's part of our DNA. But how often do we really use these empathetic instincts? Some of us are more attuned to them than others. The

---

15   Patrick Lencioni, *The Ideal Team Player*, p158.

rest of us must make a conscious choice to be more empathetic.

It's important that you think about how others are feeling on your team, especially as a result of your actions and decisions. If you are not sure, ask. Caring about others will develop your relationships with your team, leading to greater trust and a willingness from people to do more.

Ethics

The New Zealand All Blacks rugby team is arguably the best team of their kind. Their record speaks for itself – they top the tables of most statistics in the game, however you decide to cut the cake. By that definition, they are the most successful team in rugby, if not all sports.

But it's much more than that. The All Blacks have developed an almost mythical culture, built on the values and history that the team is steeped in. Generations of players have come and gone and done what the team demands – leave the jersey in a better place than when you were given it.

James Kerr was given exclusive behind the scenes access to the All Blacks for five weeks in 2010. The result is an excellent book called *Legacy: What the All Blacks can teach us about the business of life* which, for anyone interested in teams and leadership, is a must-read.

He talks about the All Blacks' culture and the need to have people on the team who are going to fit with it. Putting it simply, the All Blacks has a 'No Dickheads' policy.[16]

I love the simplicity of the word. It speaks volumes. We don't want anyone who is a dickhead. We want people who are humble and meet our code of ethics. Our ethos. Our values. Our culture. People who have running through them the values that are such a basic need of any team, we don't even have to speak them or put them up on the wall. People who are honest. People who are fair. People who don't lie or cheat or bully others. People able to admit if they are wrong or have failed. No dickheads. If you have any doubt that people don't live these basic values every day, they have no place on your team. No team is ever going to be great if contains liars, cheats and bullies. Don't even bother starting on your journey if these people are on your bus.

You want people on your team who have a strong ethic that also fits with your team ethic. Your belief systems must be aligned. If they are not, then there will be clashes and you just won't see eye to eye.

Respect

Respect matters. Respect for your teammates, your leader, your team's purpose and respect for the other

---

16   James Kerr, *Legacy*, p83.

people and institutions you interact with outside the team.

If you don't have respect, the knock-on effect will be disastrous. You are unlikely to commit and build trust, and unlikely to do what that person asks of you. Being on a team means doing things for others, because others ask you to, all the time. If you don't respect them, how likely are you to do your best work?

Sacrifice

Great team players understand that they are part of something bigger than themselves. They buy into the idea that the bigger entity that they are a part of, the team, comes first. They sacrifice their own personal needs and wants in service of the greater need of the team. They understand that the team's success is more important, but also that the team's success *is* their success and it serves them to do things for the team. They are not egotists. They don't need to hog the limelight and are satisfied to be part of a collective endeavour.

A word of warning though – if you are someone who constantly puts others before yourself, be careful that you don't burn out or expend all your physical and emotional energy supporting your team. Make sure you also spend some time satisfying your own needs and wants. This is a balancing act and you need to find the right equilibrium.

How do I know if I am a great team player?

I would hope that you would rather be a great team player than a mediocre one. I am taking that for granted, and that I don't need to point out that the better a team player you are, the more desirable you are going to be to the teams you aspire to be part of. Once there, you are more likely to make a positive and strong contribution, influencing the success of that team, where the team's success is your success. If you want to be successful in anything you do, you should aspire to be a great team player.

How will you know if you are a great team player? The answer to this question will be obvious in part. But there are a few valuable ways to work it out. You may not have all the answers yourself – far from it. There may be one or two things you do, without thinking, that you need external input to see. These blind spots are probably the most dangerous for you as an individual, so don't just think, 'I know myself, I don't need anyone else to tell me what I am like'. Be open to constructive feedback from others as part of this assessment process. The first step is to take a good hard look at yourself.

Ask yourself

This may sound obvious, but how often do we sit down and have a meaningful, focused and honest period of reflection to think about ourselves? Especially in relation to a topic such as being the best team player we can be. Find some 'me time' to do this properly, alone, where you won't be distracted. Read this chapter and have a good long think. Look at yourself in the mirror and ask yourself what you think. Do I have a high level of commitment to the tasks I undertake? Am I humble? Do I have empathy? Am I ethical? Am I a dickhead? You will know many of the answers already, if you are prepared to be honest with yourself when you do look in the mirror.

Ask other people

It's a good idea to have other people, who know you, share what they think about your skill set and attributes. If you are going to do this, you have to prepare yourself to receive feedback you may not immediately like. I know this is emotional ground, because what you are doing is asking someone else to share what they think about you. And we all take that personally, because it's about us, and not the work we do. It's easier to accept criticism of our work. It's harder when it is about who we are as people.

The other thing you must do is ask people who know you well, who are going to be objective and whom you trust. Pretty obvious, but just have a think about whom you ask. They could be a peer on the team, a friend or close family member, a coach or mentor, a leader or even your subordinate, depending on that person and the relationship you have with them. Each may give different perspectives and notice different things about you. I'd say the more the merrier, but don't overburden yourself with lots of different conversations.

The best feedback will come from those who know you well and with whom you have a high degree of trust. These people may see your blind spots, the things you don't know you are lacking, or that you are doing that you shouldn't. These could be valuable insights, and it's the ones you won't want to hear that you should pay most attention to, because these will be the ones you need to work on and change.

Assessment tools

There are several different assessment tools that you can use if you are interested. Tried and tested favourites of mine include the Myers Briggs Type Indicator (MBTI), DiSC, Gallup Strengths or Hogan Assessments. Pat Lencioni has a simple one-page assessment tool you can take based upon the competencies he covers in his book *The Ideal Team Player*.[17]

Don't forget that the true value of things like this is not in the cost of undertaking the assessment, but in the discussion and actions you take afterwards to make positive change.

---

17 Patrick Lencioni, *The Ideal Team Player*, p192.

Why should I care if I am a great team player or not?

Is all this stuff that important? Do I have to bother? Well, no, you don't, but I would think seriously about choosing not to care, and not wanting to do your best to be a great team player. Here's why.

Life is getting more collaborative

We have always worked in teams, but, as we looked at earlier, the way we live and work is getting more and more collaborative. We are more connected and reliant on others than we have ever been, and that's only going to keep growing.

Teamwork is increasingly agile

Coupled with this closer collaboration is the fluidity of work. Companies are restructuring to become far more fluid and responsive organisms. Workers are being expected to move around the company and work on different teams for shorter periods to address specific needs. As you move from team to team, there will be an expectation to quickly get up to speed and work effectively. Good team skills will allow you to integrate more smoothly and quickly into a new team.

Your career development

In the context of this agility of teamwork, you will be under constant assessment for suitability to work on different teams and projects. Team leaders will be looking for good people who they know can perform and contribute and have 'the right stuff'. The CHEERS attributes are applicable to any team and any task, so if you are good at them, you are going to increase your chances of being the one picked to be on teams and seeing progression in your career.

The team's success is your success

Great team players understand the relationship between the team's success and their own success. That is, they are intrinsically linked. The more you contribute to the success of the team, the more you contribute to your own success. Success could come in lots of different ways, and might be subtle or pay off in the longer term rather than immediately, but this relationship works. The more you put in, the better a team player you are, and the more it benefits you.

The value of team skills over technical ability

A strong set of team skills is becoming increasingly valuable to teams and employers. More and more companies and organisations are understanding that a strong team player is more important than a good résumé or technical ability. Skills like your ability to listen, take constructive feedback and solve problems are being prized over where you went to university. The CEO of LeadMD, Justin Gray, said in an article in *Inc. Magazine*: 'Résumés featuring Ivy League schools, past positions with top tier organizations, fancy logos, job titles, and impressive tech skills – they all mean nothing. I immediately file résumés in the trash.'[18] Non-traditional opportunities to develop the soft or life skills necessary for strong teamwork are on the increase. Companies are investing more and more in soft skills training, and there are organisations like Barclays Life Skills or the School of Life which offer training in these skills.

The point is, people are realising more and more that being a good team player is more valuable now than a résumé packed full of technical ability.

You can always learn technical skills

A few years ago, some friends of mine renovated an old concrete cowshed in the UK. Vicky is a Pilates instructor; Ed is a chef. Despite having no building experience, they did most of it themselves. OK, they had help with the jobs that were beyond them, like putting the roof beams in place using a crane, but they

---

18 Justin Gray, 'The single most powerful question to ask in an interview', *Inc.com*, 2017, www.inc.com/justin-gray/the-single-most-powerful-question-to-ask-in-an-int.html, accessed 28 February 2020.

did pretty much everything else. They were featured on the TV show *Grand Designs*. In it, the presenter asked Ed how he was going to do this, if he'd never done anything like it before? His response was no, he hadn't, but he was going to learn how by watching YouTube.[19] I am pleased to report that he did learn the skills and they have a stunning (and structurally sound!) home.

The ability and opportunity to learn has been revolutionised by the Internet. Sites like Google and YouTube allow you to find answers to nearly anything within a matter of minutes. Organisations like the Khan Academy are giving information away for free or next to nothing. Now we understand more about the way the brain learns, we are creating tools that tap into this knowledge to allow us to retain or access information better than ever before.

The point is, if you have a gap in a technical skill needed to do your job, you can plug it relatively quickly and easily. It is harder to plug gaps in soft skills and personality – the skills of a great team player. It can be done, and half the job is awareness of where your gaps are, but the point is that people are aware of how they can fix a gap in technical skills far quicker than one in their personal skills. If you plug those gaps and develop yourself into a great team player,

---

19 'TV Home: Cowshed conversion in Somerset', *Grand Designs Magazine*, www.granddesignsmagazine.com/grand-designs-houses/22-tv-home-cowshed-conversion-in-somerset, accessed 28 February 2020.

you are going to be more attractive to the people who will decide whether they want you on their team.

Do you pick your eight best, or your best eight?

The universities of Oxford and Cambridge have one of the greatest sporting rivalries in the world. Each year since 1829 for the men and 1927 for the women, the institutions' top boat crews have gone head-to-head in a race over a four-mile stretch of the River Thames in London. The rivalry is intense. The young men and women who are picked to be the eight rowers in each boat have got there through commitment to a punishing training regime over a period of years, to spend approximately fifteen minutes giving everything they have to beat the other boat.

Winning is everything. Failure is crushing. The actor Hugh Laurie rowed for Cambridge in 1980, narrowly losing to Oxford by just five feet. He has spoken of the 'bitter defeat' and how 'to this day [I] wouldn't want to give any pleasure or satisfaction to the opposing crew.'[20]

Who do you pick to be in the boat? There's a whole squad of rowers vying for one of those coveted eight seats and a chance for victory. They spend the whole season building up to that single race. All are

---

20 Paul Challen, *The House that Hugh Laurie Built*, p11.

supremely talented. Coaches pore over the data that is collected from countless hours spent on the rowing machines looking for paper-thin differences in ability between one rower and another, desperate to make the right choice for the crew on the day. This is where it gets interesting.

Mark de Rond is an ethnographer who works at Cambridge University's Judge Business School. He spent weeks studying the Cambridge crew to work out what constitutes the best team in a high-performance culture. De Rond says, 'What's interesting is that it seems that the eight fastest individual rowers don't make the fastest eight, the fastest boat.'[21]

De Rond is describing the concept of picking people because they have the right team skills over their technical competence. The coaches don't pick the eight rowers who are individually the best rowers, but the rowers who are going to be the best eight people to work together with each other.

You need to pick a team that can be greater than the sum of its individual parts. To do this, you need to pick people with the right character, mindset and team skills first, over and above the technical ability you are considering them for. Be careful of the maverick

---

21 Cambridge University, 'Cambridge ideas – The Boat Race: A perfect crew?', 2009, www.youtube.com/watch?v=MXLg9nsuo9I, accessed 28 February 2020.

egotist who might be extremely talented, but could
end up doing more harm than good in your team.

Balance

One vital quality you should also be looking to achieve
when putting your team together is balance. Don't fill
your team with people who have the same skills. You
need to recruit a balanced team, not only in terms of
skills, but also personality. You need a healthy mix of
introverts and extroverts, analytical thinkers and creative idea generators, for example. If your team members are similar, you are missing the opportunity to
benefit from variety, and all that this can achieve. You
will also be able to tap into people's different abilities
with a balanced team.

Do men or women make better team players?

This is an interesting question. Of course, we can't
make a sweeping generalisation, but some evidence
suggests that women have a higher level of empathy than men, and empathy is of clear benefit to your
team. A simple test called the 'reading the mind in the
eyes' test was developed by Professor Simon Baron-
Cohen at Cambridge University. He tested subjects'
ability to correctly tell someone's mood by just looking at their eyes, through showing them photographs

of the eyes of a person and asking them to guess their mood. Women scored better than men in this test.

Women may also have a higher sense of social intelligence – the ability to read groups and navigate the complexities of group interactions and relationships. Studies have shown that the more women that are in a team, the more successful it is, although some data shows that this factor peaks before you get to a 100% female group.[22]

The charismatic connector

Sandy Pentland heads up the Massachusetts Institute of Technology's Media Lab. Pentland and his colleagues at MIT have been able to apply scientific methods and innovation to study and measure the effect of good or bad teamwork.

How did they do this? As well as collecting data, they invented and developed a device called a 'sociometric badge'. This was worn around the neck like a building access card, and measured several things about what the person wearing them was up to during any given day: how they interacted with others, their tone of voice, body language, how much they listened, spoke or interrupted and how empathetic or extroverted

---

22 Anita Woolley and Thomas Malone, 'Defend your research: What makes a team smarter? More women', *Harvard Business Review*, 2011, https://hbr.org/2011/06/defend-your-research-what-makes-a-team-smarter-more-women, accessed 28 February 2020.

they were. Pentland referred to their outputs as 'socio-metrics'. [23]

The badges did not measure the actual words the team member was using. This led Pentland's team to an important discovery – in high-performing teams, what was being said was less important than the *way* it was being said.

Sandy's team also tested a hypothesis around the concept of an ideal team player. They worked out that there are certain characteristics that make up this person – someone they called a 'charismatic connector'. Charismatic connectors were found to circulate actively, and their conversations were often high-energy exchanges. They shared their time equally between team members. Interestingly, they were not always extroverted personalities, but they were all confident to approach and engage with others. Pentland also observed that charismatic connectors spent as much or more time listening as they did talking; a trait he termed 'energized but focused listening'.

'The best team players also connect their teammates with one another and spread ideas around. In a study of executives attending an intensive one-week executive education class at MIT, we found that the more of these

23   Alex 'Sandy' Pentland, 'The new science of building great teams', *Harvard Business Review*, 2012, https://hbr.org/2012/04/the-new-science-of-building-great-teams, accessed 28 February 2020.

charismatic connectors a team had, the more successful it was.'[24]

What I find most interesting about the concept of charismatic connectors is that it does not matter what you are saying. The words themselves are secondary to the behaviour, and that focused listening is as important as talking. This has been corroborated in other studies like Google's Project Aristotle which we will hear more about in the next chapter. The point is, good team players are ones that connect well with others around them. It is worth asking yourself whether you are truly a charismatic connector, or could you be better at this? And can you be a better listener?

---

24   Alex 'Sandy' Pentland, 'The new science of building great teams'.

FIVE
Psychological Safety

If you have been reading from the beginning of this book, you may have picked up that we have been making a journey through time. Your team starts with an idea – a reason for being, something that it needs to do. Then you start out on that journey, deciding your purpose and compelling goals, picking who is going to be part of the team, who will be in charge and how they will successfully lead it. You are ready to go. But what should you do next?

Teams need to create the right atmosphere, culture or ethos that will be conducive to both their enjoyment of their work and also their success at it. Things like behavioural norms, rituals and actions, language and history will form part of your team's culture. But the most essential thing that every team needs is an atmosphere that is psychologically safe.

What is psychological safety?

Psychological safety is the behavioural climate in a team, which dictates how people act and react when interaction and communication take place. It dictates to what extent people feel able to speak up, and the level of interpersonal fear. Do your team members keep quiet for fear of being judged, laughed at or ridiculed for what they say? Do they fear an angry, triggered reaction to their words?

According to Amy Edmondson, Professor of Leadership and Management at Harvard Business School, a psychologically safe climate 'makes it possible to give tough feedback and have difficult conversations without the need to tiptoe around the truth.'[25] Teams where this doesn't exist are walking through a minefield of destructive possibilities, bound to shatter any chances of achieving greatness. If people are shackled by a fear of speaking up, then either they will do poor work, or the work won't happen at all.

Don't underestimate how important it is to create a safe culture and environment in your team, from the very start. Psychological safety is a code of behaviour, a standard, an expectation and a rule that you need to

---

25   Amy Edmondson, *Teaming*, p118.

create and absolutely insist on in your team. This is something that should be a given and should be lived in how you interact with each other, every day. Failure to create this environment will have serious implications on the possibilities of success and the level of pain or pleasure that you will experience in your day-to-day existence as a team.

Why do you need to have psychological safety?

We all know Google to be an innovative and ambitious company with a curious approach. In 2012, Google embarked on Project Aristotle to satisfy the curiosity they had about teamwork, or more specifically, what makes a *great* team? Of course, they had a vested interest in answering this question for their own benefit, but we are fortunate that we can all benefit from this research.

Their research was exhaustive. Not only did they study hundreds of their own teams, but they reviewed practically all the academic studies that had been done into team dynamics over the past fifty years. What was interesting in this research was the common initial assumption that it was *who* was on a team that mattered, and the skills, capabilities and make-up of those people mattered most.

Soon, though, the interviews and research pointed towards a different conclusion. It wasn't who was on the team that mattered, but the *way* some teams interacted and behaved that was a higher predictor of success.

The researchers who conducted Project Aristotle identified five key characteristics that high-performing teams displayed. At the top of this list was the need for psychological safety to exist. This was by far the biggest predictor of a team's success. Everything flowed from there. Once a team had that, then they could expect dependability, structure and clarity, and could create meaning and impact.[26]

It is said that high-performance teamwork begins with developing trust, and this is true. But what I like about the Google model is that it addresses something deeper than that. Something must exist first in order for trust to be able to develop. A condition, an environment, a culture, which will allow it to develop in the first place. This is what we call psychological safety.

Trust only grows when people talk. If you are fearful of being judged or ridiculed and don't want to be vulnerable and open yourself up to criticism, then you are not going to speak up. And if you don't speak up, then people aren't going to get to know things about

---

26 Charles Duhigg, 'What Google learned from its quest to build the perfect team', *New York Times*, 2016, www.nytimes.com/2016/02/28/magazine/what-google-learned-from-its-quest-to-build-the-perfect-team.html, accessed 28 February 2020.

you. You don't have to become friends In teams – Google's research proved that – but you have to trust one another and have respect for one another. Am I going to trust you if I have a suspicion that you will laugh at me? Am I going to respect you if I don't know how you will behave in each situation, or whether or not you are reliable? Absolutely not, on both counts.

This is why a pre-existing condition of psychological safety is vitally important to great teamwork. All that other good stuff that needs to happen won't germinate if you don't have this in place.

As Charles Duhigg says in his *New York Times* article on the project: 'To be fully present at work, to feel "psychologically safe", we must know that we can be free enough, sometimes, to share things that scare us without fear of recriminations. We must be able to talk about what is messy or safe, to have hard conversations with colleagues who are driving us crazy.'[27]

Psychological safety – the challenge

Creating a psychologically safe environment takes bravery. It may not be easy. It will require potentially brutal honesty. People may need to be told things they don't want to hear. There will be conflict, even argument. There will probably be times when you will be

---

27 Charles Duhigg, 'What Google learned from its quest to build the perfect team'.

tempted to chicken out of that tough conversation and think, 'Anything for an easy life'. But this is the coward's way out. All that will do is perpetuate the damaging conditions that a lack of psychological safety brings.

You may be shying away from the idea of creating a psychologically safe environment because your team doesn't have one now, and the thought of how exposing this whole concept is fills you with dread. You'd rather not do the heavy lifting required and instead put up with what you currently have. 'Better the devil you know.'

If you take this route, you are going down a path where your team will always be experiencing a level of pain. I'll come on to what happens when there isn't psychological safety, but in the extreme, it is highly damaging and even has an impact on people's physical health. It is where stress thrives, and increasingly we are understanding how damaging stress can be to the body and mind.

I urge you to take on the challenge of creating a climate of psychological safety, not because we should all aspire to be great, to be the best in the world, the best at what we do – no, I urge you to take this on because it is the fundamental state that teams and the people within them deserve. It doesn't matter if you are attempting to scale Everest or to just go for a Sunday afternoon stroll. Whatever your goal, this is more about the pain factor you will experience if you don't make psychological safety indispensable to your team.

I especially challenge those of you who are tempted to say, 'I am not prepared to do this. It's too exposing. Too difficult. Too scary. I don't want to be great. I just want an easy life'. It's OK if you decide that you don't want to reach Everest. You might have a small business and you are happy with that. We don't all have to be Google, Virgin, Toyota or Apple. But I strongly feel that, however big or small your ambition, creating a psychologically safe environment is not only the first step towards success, it is something that I feel every human being who works in a team has the right to expect.

Psychological safety is where trust and respect are born. It's where relationships and friendships are built. Where interdependence, collaboration and support happen. Teams that have a high level of psychological safety will create higher morale, have more fun, be populated by people who give more to each other and sacrifice more in the interest of the team's happiness and success. No matter where you work or what your team does, how big or small it is, and where it's going, you should expect as a basic human right to have these working conditions. And if you put these in place, then you are only going to increase your chance of success.

Don't settle. Don't shy away from the tough conversations and decisions that are necessary for you to move towards a psychologically safe environment for your team to live and work in. The consequences of doing so are too painful and damaging. Trust me, I've worked in and with teams that are at both ends of the psychological safety scale, and I know how bad or good it can be – and when it's good, the rewards can be great.

What happens when you don't have psychological safety?

This question could be asked in two ways. What are the bad things that *do* happen, and what are the good things that *don't* happen in a psychologically unsafe environment?

Silence

The most common issue that arises is people don't speak up. In her book *Teaming*, Amy Edmondson talks about the problem of 'groupthink', which occurs when people don't want to upset the apple cart and speak out or give their opinion. Maybe the team is in a good place, where everyone is rubbing along nicely and on the surface everything seems OK. But this belies what is really going on. Edmondson identifies the phenomenon in which individuals within cohesive teams can feel reluctant to cause disharmony when there appears to be agreement on an important issue, and so hold back views which might be seen to create dissent in the group. This 'groupthink' leads to poor decision-making.[28]

Lack of trust and respect

As we've already learnt, the essential qualities of trust and respect struggle to be developed when psychological safety is missing. Even greater than that, mistrust and disdain can appear within a team, a sure-fire sign of unhappiness. Silence makes this worse. If people are not talking, they are not developing knowledge of each other, they are not developing the experiences required to allow people to see trustworthiness. They will default to mistrust as an instinct for fear of the unknown.

Indecision and time-wasting

As well as making the wrong decisions, a lack of psychological safety will mean your team is likely to be indecisive and waste time. People will skirt around issues, use delaying tactics to avoid conflict, or waste time going through a lengthier process of decision-making than would be necessary if they were being honest and upfront in the first place.

---

28   Amy Edmondson, *Teaming*, p119.

Blame

Blame is an entirely unproductive exercise. It's draining and a highly negative thing to do and is all too present in teams without psychological safety. Blame does still happen in teams with high levels of psychological safety, but it is more likely to be present in teams without it. Why? Because people often leap to blame others when they are either not in possession of all the facts or are keen to find a scapegoat because they fear the wrath and judgement coming their way if they don't.

Lack of risk-taking

Teams have different attitudes towards risk and reward, but all need to take some form of risk at some point. If we only ever took the 100% safe route, we'd be unlikely to get very far. It is necessary, especially if you want to achieve great things. Teams of people fearing the consequences of action are far less likely to take a risk and, therefore, to make great achievements.

The rumour mill

Energy spent discussing, listening to or spreading rumours is wasted. If everyone is informed, there is no gap to be filled with salacious gossip about what is going on. Like blame, rumour-mongering goes on in the best of teams, but it is more likely to exist in psychologically unsafe environments where there are these gaps. Psychological safety doesn't have to mean everyone knows everything, but that team members are happy with the amount of knowledge they do have.

Rumours and gossip also come about because people are desperate to have information they can use as a weapon. It's terrible to think of teams where this condition exists, where people feel it necessary to arm themselves with information they can use to defend themselves against or to attack other people in the team.

Lack of innovation

Great innovation comes from an environment of openness that allows for creativity and experimentation to take place. Imagine you are in a team where you are trying to innovate a new product or service, and you feel you are going to be judged by others, or your ideas are going to be laughed at. How likely are you to speak up with a really 'out there' idea? Not very.

Innovation demands an open-minded approach. 'No' should not be in your vocabulary when you are carrying out an innovation process. People must feel safe to come up with ideas. To challenge each other, to play devil's advocate, to debate and refine is essential to creating ideas. This simply won't happen if people are spending time and mental space thinking about the potential for judgement and ridicule rather than focusing on new ideas that might seem a bit silly, but could lead to great innovation.

What if I fear the consequences of trying to develop psychological safety?

I sense hesitation when I talk to teams about developing psychological safety. What we are talking about here can feel threatening. As you read this, you might be fearing the consequences of attempting to develop a climate of psychological safety in your own team. Some teams will already have a healthy climate, or be part of the way there, but for a lot of you, this will be a real challenge. The thought of broaching the subject of psychological safety and the fall-out from tough conversations might be too much to contemplate.

I get it. Why? Because I am a person who doesn't like argument and heated debate. I naturally shy away from entering into these situations where voices are raised and emotions run high. These are not my comfort zones. I know a lot of people feel the same. My fight or flight instincts kick in and I can't wait for the situation to end. This may be something that you are feeling when you consider what you might have to go through to reach psychological safety on your team.

As human beings we are flawed, imperfect and liable to emotionally highjack ourselves. Emotions may leap to the surface from time to time, especially as you begin the process. But you must accept this. Be prepared for it.

Once I became aware of my personal attitude towards emotional and aggressive argument, I was able to accept it is just how I am. I am always going to react to those situations, so I have learnt to not take them personally and to forge through the barriers preventing me from making a meaningful contribution.

You must not be scared of conflict. Conflict is a prerequisite of good teamwork. Healthy conflict is preferable, where people enter into meaningful, honest debate that is handled with maturity and controlled emotion. But I'd rather almost *any* conflict than none at all. There is a line you shouldn't cross, where things get ugly, and certainly it shouldn't descend into anything physical. But sometimes blowing out cobwebs with a bit of a shout turns out to be a good thing.

If your hesitation around developing psychological safety is about raised voices and argument, then like me, you just need to learn how to deal with it. You have to compartmentalise those fight or flight desires and see them as necessary to the process.

In 1965, Dr Bruce Tuckman published his team development model that talks about the stages you go through when you create a team – the forming, storming, norming and performing phases[29]. Teams pass through the first three stages in order to get to where they can really perform. Forming is the initial phase of identifying the aim and goals and who is on the team, when the team is getting ready for launch. The storming is the phase where everyone is working each other out, agreements on behaviour begin to get established, hierarchy, roles and responsibilities are worked out and so on. It's called storming because it can be stormy! There can be misunderstanding and a lack of clarity as everything is getting worked out, but it can also be quite exciting.

Norming is where things from the storming phase get resolved, trust and intimacy are built, and acceptance is created. From there, the team can move forward to really performing what they are there to do, because everything about the team in theory is in place.

Introducing or developing psychological safety might create a fair bit of storming before you get to norming. Ideally, you'll have minimal fuss but be prepared for it to happen. I'll come on to ways you can develop psychological safety that minimise the potential for conflict, but if it happens, see it as simply part of the process in reaching a new normal for your team.

---

29 Bruce Tuckman, 'Developmental sequence in small groups', *Psychological Bulletin*, 63 (6), 1965, pp384–99.

What if people leave?

You may fear the staffing consequences of developing psychological safety, especially in a team where it doesn't exist currently. What if the process is too much for people and they decide to leave? Can we live without them if they have crucial skills or knowledge that we would rather not do without?

Let me be clear about this. This is one of the most important points I will make in this entire book: *Anyone who is not prepared to exist in a team that expects them to accept a psychologically safe environment should not be on that team.*

Psychological safety is that important. It is a prerequisite of any team that harbours a desire to reach any goal with as little pain as possible along the way. It is a deal breaker. A foundation stone. A pillar. A team is bigger than any individual within it, and if someone isn't prepared to live with the values and behaviours associated with psychological safety – honesty, trust, interdependency, humility, and putting the needs of the team and other people on it before their own – then they don't belong on your team.

I have said that high-performance teamwork isn't going to be easy. It takes bravery. Soul searching. Honesty – not only with others, but also with yourself. Any fear you might be experiencing around what happens if people leave is natural. Many of us don't like upsetting the status quo. Especially if that person is highly talented to the point of genius or holds essential information in their head. But I would urge you to also ask the question, 'What if they *don't* leave?' What happens then?

In Liz Wiseman's book *Multipliers*, she tells the story of KR Sridhar, leader of Bloom Energy, a Silicon Valley company that developed a clean, reliable and affordable fuel cell system. They had some tough goals to achieve against tight deadlines. There was no time to spare.

On Sridhar's team was one indispensable scientist, a world expert on the technology they needed to develop. But this guy was a problem. He wasn't able to collaborate and was stubbornly fixated on a course of action that Sridhar and the team felt wasn't the right way to go.

People feared life without this scientist. They considered him essential to their chances of success. The scientist in question had a 'my way or the highway' mentality, giving Sridhar a difficult call to make. In the end, he chose the team over the individual and asked that person to leave.

Sridhar knew this decision would be a shock and that it would produce fear, but he felt sure it was the right course of action. He explained things to the team, that this would mean they faced an even steeper uphill struggle, but he was confident they could still do it. Sure enough, the team pulled together and completed the eight-month project with only a two-day delay in meeting the deadline.

Wiseman's research consistently shows that people like Sridhar's scientist – whom she terms 'diminishers' – 'cause people to operate at about 50 percent of their full intelligence and capability… On a work team of eleven people, removing a diminisher can give back the equivalent of five full time people, with ten people operating at 100 percent.'[30]

This is living by the creed of psychological safety. Don't be afraid to make this kind of tough decision, if someone is standing in the way of your team working and living in a safe psychological environment. In the long run, with careful management and a commitment to plugging the gap they leave with whatever needs to be done, you will reap the benefits.

How to create a psychologically safe environment

I hope by now you are a fully paid up member of the psychological safety fan club and want to make sure your team is living and breathing this concept every day. No matter where you are on the scale of having none or a lot on your team already, there's work to do.

30   Liz Wiseman, *Multipliers*, p54.

There is one important thing you need to know. You can't impose psychological safety on teams – it must be something that people understand and want to be a part of. For those who want it, you have to bring it home and make it tangible for them. It's an abstract concept, so work hard to make it real and directly applicable to each person in your team.

This is not going to be a one-stage process. You can't expect people to 'get it' with one chat or email to suddenly become psychologically safe. This is going to take time and effort. Like a multichannel marketing campaign, a mix of strategies and tools will be needed. But it's worth the investment of time and resource, as it is so important to your wellbeing and success as a team.

Here are some tips for developing psychological safety within your team.

Leaders lead the way

As for any process of change, it is vital that leaders not only buy into the whole concept and permit it to happen, but that they take the initiative in leading the way. As Amy Edmondson says, 'The most important influence on psychological safety is the nearest manager, supervisor or boss.'[31] I can't tell you how many times I have seen teams try to make changes and the

---

31   Amy Edmondson, *Teaming*, p137.

top management either don't care or are not even present in the room where their teams are working on that change. If it's not important enough to them and they aren't present, what sort of message does that send to the people lower down the chain? I have refused to work with clients whose leader won't take part in the change programme or coaching session they asked me to work with them on. I cannot help them change if the leader isn't interested or present. The first step is to engage the leadership to agree and instigate the process.

Generate understanding of what psychological safety is

Don't try to introduce a potentially radical idea without preparing the ground first. A farmer doesn't just scatter seeds anyhow on a field. He takes the time to plough, weed and fertilise it before even thinking about planting them, to give them the best chance of growing. You need to make sure that everyone on your team knows what psychological safety is, what it looks like and what it's going to feel like. You will potentially be provoking people to think about some fairly revealing behaviour by introducing psychological safety. This may put them on edge, but they will be more likely to get on board with the rest of the team if they have some time to reflect and get ready for the change ahead.

There are various ways to do this. Get them to read this chapter, for starters. You can share articles, videos from YouTube – there's a great one where Charles Duhigg summarises Project Aristotle, for example[32] – and any other material you can find. You can hold education sessions, which you can run with your own team, or you could engage the services of an external facilitator or coach to generate discussion and learning around the topic.

Focus the team's effort on how psychological safety works specifically for them

Psychological safety may be seen as an abstract or theoretical idea. Without its practical application to your team's everyday activity, there might be a disconnect and people won't make the necessary changes to their behaviour. It's all well and good talking about it to teams and getting them to understand the concept, but you have to work on the practical implementation of behavioural change for it to become the new way of life. If you have done a great job of introducing psychological safety to the team and educating them about it, you have to make the implementation of the policy directly relevant to them. You should ensure they can understand exactly how it affects their situation and the mechanics of how they need to behave differently as a result. If you do not take it beyond

---

32 Tech Insider, 'How Google builds the perfect team', 2016, www. youtube.com/watch?v=v2PaZ8Nl2T4, accessed 28 February 2020.

theory into practice, it may not really take hold within the organisation.

How often have you seen a table football game in an office? This is often proudly shown off as you walk past it by the person you are visiting, as a shining example of the great culture the company has. But does it really change behaviour? Sadly, all too often organisations make token gestures like this that they think are going to make everything different, but they don't do the real work to make it happen. Don't fall into the trap of creating a lot of hot air and superficial gestures that don't get to the meat of the problem or really resonate with the team every day.

This is a crucial point. Nearly everyone is going to understand the concept, and want to have a psycho-logically safe environment, but there might be some head scratching over exactly *how* to achieve it. It is important that you connect the initiative with real actions. You need to focus on the actual work and dif-ferent, specific behaviours people need to adopt for the new climate to be created.

Get people's buy-in

Everyone's voice needs to be heard on this topic. You need to invite each team member to weigh in and say what they think – after all, this is the basic premise of psychological safety. This doesn't have to mean that they stand up in front of others and talk about what they are feeling and thinking. The idea of doing that will scare most people into silence. Public speaking is rated as one of the top fears for people; in a 2001 Gallup survey asking a group of American adults about their fears, speaking in front of an audience was ranked second only to snakes, with 40% of people naming it as their greatest fear.[33] So, don't expect everyone to speak up, as although some extroverts will be happy to do so, the introverts on your team will be quaking in their boots.

To allow the introverts a voice, you can ask for their input in writing. If you are discussing psychological safety in a meeting, for example, give people a chance to write down what they think and feel first – maybe on sticky notes they can put on the board – before you open it up to group discussion. Allow smaller, more intimate discussion sessions or tabletop discussions rather than asking everyone to speak up in front of the whole group. Outside of a meeting, you could encourage them to share their thoughts by email or anonymous survey.

Whatever methods and channels you use, you need to make sure that everyone knows that this is a 'cards on the table' discussion. Absolute honesty is a must. People cannot have a hidden agenda, lie or hold back. If they don't buy in and communicate their thoughts or

---

33 Geoffrey Brewer, 'Snakes top list of Americans' fears', *Gallup*, 2001, https://news.gallup.com/poll/1891/snakes-top-list-americans-fears.aspx, accessed 4 March 2020.

feelings now, it will hurt them in the long run. That's the kind of message you need to send, because you now expect people to think and act with absolute honesty every day, and you have done from the moment you decided to make psychological safety a priority in your organisation and team.

Having this healthy discussion will elicit debate and potentially conflicting opinions. But the important thing is, everyone's opinion will have been heard, which is vital if you are going to get them to buy into creating a psychologically safe way of working.

Ask people directly

I learnt a big leadership lesson once. I always had an open-door policy with my team and used to say, 'If you have a problem or concern, please come and tell me about it'. I assumed that people would do so, and therefore believed everyone was fine because people were not coming to me with a problem. I was always surprised when I would ask directly in their quarterly or annual review 'Is everything OK?' and they would respond with something along the lines of 'Well, now you ask, I have this issue…'

It was frustrating. I would always think, 'If you had this issue, why didn't you come and tell me about it?' But it's a classic case of 'If you don't ask, you won't get'. It's simple but effective. You have to ask people directly if they will make the behavioural changes you need from them to increase psychological safety.

Clearly outline what you expect of them, how you want them to behave and what you want them to do, then ask for their commitment. I urge you to do this face-to-face. Don't send a group email or make a phone call. Get someone in front of you to ask, 'Will you?' A study was done at Cornell that shows you are thirty-four times more likely to get a positive response if you ask in person.[34]

I also advocate asking in front of others on the team. What you are trying to do here is secure commitment so you can hold people accountable. There's something powerful in getting people to commit to something within earshot of others. Even if those other people aren't directly involved in whatever it is your team member is committing to, or that person is not directly accountable to them, it's just a human behavioural trait. If other people know we've said yes to something, even if those people aren't invested in what we've said yes to, we feel a greater pressure to do it than if we'd only said yes to one person. This is why wedding vows are said in front of the community of people most dear to us. We are making a solemn promise that they are now party to and can legitimately hold us to account for. It's powerful even

---

34 Vanessa K Bohns, 'A face-to-face request is 34 times more successful than an email', *Harvard Business Review*, 2017, https://hbr.org/2017/04/a-face-to-face-request-is-34-times-more-successful-than-an-email, accessed 28 February 2020.

if they are strangers, more powerful still if they are people on the team who will be directly affected by the consequences of the individual's action or inaction.

Be prepared to be vulnerable

Imagine you're standing on the side of a lake or pond. The water is a few feet below you. You're not standing on a cliff, but you are high enough to make the jump you are contemplating a bigger deal than jumping off the side of a swimming pool.

You look down at the water. It's murky, so you can't see more than an inch or two into it. You don't know how deep it is. You know it's safe to jump in your head, but your heart is still telling you to be careful of the unknown. You take a deep breath, close your eyes, and jump. You hit the water with shock at how cold it is and you go under, but in a second or two, you are breaking the surface. Everything is fine and you are keen to go back and have another go.

This is a metaphor for doing anything for the first time, and it certainly applies to creating an atmosphere where people are prepared to be vulnerable. People must be prepared to speak up and leave themselves open to the response of others if you expect them to admit mistakes, or if they don't know something, or if they have failed. They need to have confidence that the response will not be unkind or judgemental, but supportive and positive.

How do you take the first step when it comes to vulnerability? It's hard. This is a tough one to get right, but if you have done it once, the floodgates can open. And this is one of those situations where leaders earn their money. It's their job to go first. When I say leaders, I mean the head of department, the CEO or the team captain. But this can be one of those moments when someone takes on the mantle of leadership by being the first one who puts themselves out there. It can be one of the members of the team who takes that first step. By doing that, they are leading in that moment – and bravo to them. It takes bravery. Blind faith. Risk. But it's a risk worth taking.

People who express vulnerability endear themselves to others. Think about this for a moment. Think about a time when someone has laid themselves bare, has let down their guard and shown their honest self to you or others within your sight. How did it feel? What sort of reaction did it elicit? A lot of the time, people want to support that person. This is where our hardwiring helps us out for a change. We're social animals who thrive in communities with other humans and we have a strong instinct to protect others in our tribe who are in trouble. When someone is vulnerable, they are showing fallibility, and most of us want to help them as a result.

Protect the vulnerable

It's absolutely crucial that from the very first moment vulnerability appears within your team, you must protect, support and encourage it to grow. It's like a little plant, desperately pushing up through the soil, battling for sunlight and fighting the wind and frost. The slightest adverse condition will kill it off. Not until it has grown strong and tall and can fight for itself can you turn your back and leave it alone.

In the same way, during the early stages of a team taking the first faltering baby steps of showing vulnerability, it's everyone's responsibility to protect each other. The minute someone laughs, judges or ridicules the vulnerable, you must stamp that behaviour out immediately. Be firm on this, to the point of being prepared to lose someone who does the wrong thing here. You have to let vulnerability grow. It's the life spring of psychological safety. It gives air to the supportive, non-judgemental, accepting environment that is the ground from which grow all the good things psychological safety creates. The consequences of acting contrary to this code of behaviour should be serious.

Insist on it

Your attitude towards the development and continuation of psychological safety should be one-dimensional. There is no other way. Either you buy into this philosophy and way of being, or you are out. Insist on it as much as you insist people live your company values, perhaps more. Do not compromise on this.

Live it every day

People talk about having a practice, like meditation or yoga, that they do regularly. Psychological safety should be something you practise every day so that it becomes a way of life. Your team has to consciously do it until it becomes second nature. Be vulnerable. Speak up. Be honest. Don't judge. Support. Don't have hidden agendas. Don't gossip. Allow mistakes and failure. Banish fear. All of these are part of the practice of psychological safety. Get everyone's buy-in to the concept and get everyone's shoulder to the proverbial wheel. It might take conscious effort to start with, but this is what happens when you need to make a change in behaviour.

Do it every day. Celebrate it when you see it happening and come down hard when you see people breaking the code. Remember to reward in public and reprimand in private. Don't tear people off a strip in front of others. That will only be counterproductive. Everyone should feel responsible. Everyone can say 'Well done!' and 'Thank you!' when they see it happening and as long as it's done constructively, everyone should feel able to challenge anyone who goes against it – especially the leader. One of the signs of a healthy team is a leader who accepts feedback from the people below them.

SIX
Communication

The importance of communication

When I first work with a team, I like to know what I am working with in terms of the maturity of the group's thinking and knowledge of teamwork. This helps me decide where I need to start – do I need to go back to basics and educate them, or are they quite advanced, so we can focus on a particular area for their development? I ask questions like, 'What does teamwork mean to you?' and 'What does good teamwork look like?'

Usually, the first words that come out include one of the most important aspects of effective teamwork: 'Communication'. People know that communication is key. Teamwork is all about working interdependently with others towards a common goal. Intrinsic to that is the need to communicate thoughts, suggest ideas, give advice or dictate instructions to others on the team. We have to share our knowledge, report on what we are doing, debate issues to make decisions and create commitment, solve problems or receive affirmation that what we are doing is right. Communication does all of this and more, and for this reason is one of the most essential skills teams need to get right.

But as much as the people know communication is important, more often than not they can't clearly articulate why, or how they do it, or say confidently whether they are getting it right or wrong. We rarely actually think about it, or consider working on it as a skill, like we do with leadership or sales or other learning and development areas that companies spend a lot of time and money developing.

Without communication, teamwork can't happen, so without great communication, great teamwork can't happen. Many aspects of teamwork – things like trust, respect, purpose, morale, clarity – do not need to be present to their fullest extent for the team to get by. You can still do teamwork without a strong compelling purpose, or you can work with people if trust isn't present. It won't be pretty, and you won't be very successful, but you can get by. But communication has to be there, which is why it is so essential.

I am sure you have had conversations with a team-mate – be it with someone at work, with your spouse or with a player on your sports team – where you are thinking carefully about what you say and how you say it. Maybe you are giving some delicate feedback about room for improvement, breaking some upsetting news or trying to persuade a demotivated person to turn things around. Your choice of words, tone of voice, even hand gestures are absolutely crucial to get right. The conversation could go one of two ways, depending entirely on how you act in that interaction. We all face moments like this working in teams, where your communication skills need to be firing on all cylinders.

Communication is vital for ensuring clarity. If you don't communicate, then you are leaving gaps in knowledge that people will fill with assumption and conjecture. If you don't have frequent opportunities to share information about what's happening with the team now and in the future, people are going to worry or make it up themselves. We fill voids because voids are the unknown, and as we've seen before, we fear the unknown. Not speaking can be more damaging than saying the wrong thing. How often do we overthink an issue when we are not in possession of all the facts? 'I wonder if she likes me'. 'Is my job safe?' 'How will they react?' We don't like not being able to answer questions. Teams need clarity on so many things – their purpose, goals, relationships, expectations, behaviour. You need to communicate these properly to proactively fill any voids before people fall into the trap of filling them with the wrong information.

Because communication is such an everyday fact of life for us, we often don't think about the mechanics of it all. When we are so familiar with something, it's often difficult to articulate what we feel about it or to describe it accurately. Try, for example, to say why you love your husband or wife. Many of us will come up with some form of 'I don't know, it's difficult to say, I just kind of love them.'

We are also all so busy with everything taking up our brain space these days that we don't have time to stop and think about some of the basic stuff we take for granted. We don't stop and think about things like communication. Teams don't spend enough time on it. They don't realise how important it is, and therefore don't prescribe it any serious development time. Because it's like trying to describe why you love your spouse – quite an abstract concept – we don't tackle it properly in our teams. But if we don't take control of improving our communication, we leave our success or failure as communicators to chance.

The Chimp Paradox

Imagine for a moment that you are driving along on a warm summer's day, windows down, your favourite station on the radio, early for the appointment that awaits you at your destination. There's no pressure to go fast. In fact, seeing as it's a nice day, you settle back into your seat and enjoy the ride for a change.

You slow down as you approach a queue of traffic. As you do so, a car screams up the inside lane to dive into the closing gap between you and the stationary car in front, causing you to brake suddenly. You react without thinking, slamming your fist onto the horn, and shouting out a torrent of expletives that you regret the moment you see your four-year-old's shocked face in the rearview mirror. The incident made you forget they were there.

What just happened? You have been the victim of your own mind, what Dr Steve Peters calls 'The Chimp Paradox' in his book of the same title. The basic premise is this: our brains are made up of two sides, or influences. One is our conscious, rational human self, capable of calm reflection, assessment of situations and an adult reaction. The other is our animalistic, subconscious, emotional self – our chimp.

'Our inner chimp can be our best friend or our worst enemy. This is the Chimp Paradox.'[35] The chimp inside us is the legacy of our forebears, a highly instinctive part of our personality and brains. The chimp analogy is perfect – childlike, simplistic, emotional,

---

35 Steve Peters, *The Chimp Paradox* (back cover).

playful, aggressive, swift to act without thinking first. Wonderful in some respects, flawed in others.

Our chimp is highly strung and emotionally driven. Road rage is a perfect example of the chimp at work. We react instantly to a change in circumstance, a perceived threat, with our chimp. Loud, impulsive, aggressive, protective. We slam the horn and shout words we never use in normal conversation. We feel a surge of adrenalin. Our heart rate increases, pupils dilate. We might even bare our teeth. All of these are animalistic reactions to a situation we perceived as a threat. It doesn't have to be a physical threat – in this instance it was a threat to us being first. Don't under-estimate the powerful urge to win that is within us.

Once the car has pulled in and there's nothing to be done, we start to calm down. Our breathing slows, we take a deep breath. Ask yourself 'Why did you react that way? What did you gain?' The answer is, of course, nothing. There's nothing you could have done to stop that car pulling in front of you. And why should you have? You told yourself not two minutes ago you had the time to sit back and enjoy the journey. You could have let several cars go in front of you and you'd still be way ahead of time. All you've done is cause yourself stress you didn't need.

Imagine now if you'd been able to engage your rational brain. You see the car about to pull in. You quickly manage to control your emotions and remind yourself you have plenty of time. Why not let him into the line? He might be in a hurry for some reason. Do the guy a favour. How much better would that calm and measured response have been? But that is not easy. In fact, it's incredibly hard to overrule your chimp. He (or she) is primed and ready for action at a moment's notice.

Don't grab your pitchforks and go attempting to chase your chimp out of your village. You will never win. Your chimp is in your DNA. It is an inherited and essential part of your make-up. The chimp can also be your friend, can protect you from harm. After all, it is based upon all those millennia of experience your ancestors had of protecting themselves from the real and ever-present danger of predators back on the savannah. You need your chimp at times.

Imagine you are in a meeting with your team, trying to come to a decision on an important and emotive issue that you know people have different opinions on. You need to have a wide-ranging and compre-hensive debate on the issue and ultimately come to a decision together, either one that everyone agrees with or that they at least respect and commit to.

Who would you like to be present in this meeting? Would you like you and your teammates to send them-selves in, or send in their chimps? Imagine a room full of chimps. The chattering chaos as they bicker, fight and scream. The ill-discipline, lack of listening and absence of any form of respect or progress. Not only would they never get to a decision, they would tire themselves out completely in the process.

Chimps, generally speaking, are not good for teams, because an essential skill for all teams is communication. For the most part, we need to control them when it comes to working in teams and place them in the back seat while we let our adult, conscious selves do the talking.

One of the first things you need to do when working on communication in your team is to educate everyone about the concept of the inner chimp, and how destructive it can be if you let it rule how you communicate. The first step to effective communication is controlling and working with your chimp, not against it. If you all understand that they exist, are aware of their power and how they behave, then you can start to control them.

Jane and her chimp

I once managed a sales team that contained someone who could be a handful. Jane was a bit of a lone wolf who produced excellent results, but who operated privately and often rubbed people up the wrong way. She was also prone to fairly heated outbursts from time to time.

I had to give Jane some feedback on one occasion to suggest she change how she do things to prevent the conflict she was causing within the team.

I called Jane into my office and within minutes, the meeting exploded. She went on the defensive, denying any wrong-doing, accusing me of victimising her, apportioning blame to others and shouting over me. She was so overwhelmed by her chimp, that at one point she reverted to her native language, which I couldn't understand. She had been completely hijacked.

I quickly realised that Jane was in a state where she couldn't function normally. She had to calm down and get the chimp back in its cage. I told her to go away and come back in an hour, allowing time for her to regain control and think rationally about what had happened. I also needed time. It had taken a lot of self-control not to let my chimp out too, which would have been disastrous, and I needed to let the adrenalin subside and work out a way of getting through to Jane.

I also had problems with Jane's chimp when she let him out in the open plan office, where she had a dispute with a colleague that had been brewing for weeks. Finally, the issue – which, by the way, was totally made up because there was a void that each party had filled with their own preconceptions and conjecture – spilt out into the open, and the other person's chimp also took over. Two chimps going at each other is a frightening sight, especially in front of the rest of the team. It unsettles people, disrupts the equilibrium and creates a great deal of unease.

Things had reached a crisis point with Jane. Thankfully, I managed to get through to her. I liked her and she produced great results. It was just unfortunate that she was a victim of her chimp far too often. As I said earlier, you are never going to get rid of your team members' chimps and you need them in your team at times, but you need people to control them. I am happy to report that I was able to make Jane see it this way and got her to read *The Chimp Paradox*. It worked, and the results of her commitment to change were transformational. She became a far better team player and the 'chimp' issues never arose again. She continued to deliver the great results she had always done, in a more harmonious and less damaging way for her, me and the team.

Jane did two things wrong, as so many of us do in all areas of our life, not just in the context of the teams we belong to. Number one, not enough of us are even aware that we have an inner chimp who decides our thoughts and actions and creates a destructive knee-jerk reaction to circumstances before we have time to think rationally. And two, we don't control the chimp enough to prevent communication from becoming destructive, ruining the chance of achieving a pain-free existence on our teams. Everyone on your team has to be self-disciplined and keep their chimps under control, if you are to have any chance at achieving productive, meaningful and successful communication.

How to control your chimp

Controlling chimps is not easy. They come out when we are at our most vulnerable, emotionally triggered or defensive. After all, they are completely motivated by an overwhelming instinct to protect us and ensure our survival. Anytime we are remotely threatened, they start rattling at the doors of the cage. We even change physically when the chimp is out, with the release of adrenalin and blood flow being prioritised to where it's needed most.

Just being aware that our chimp exists is a significant step. Being in total control of your chimp is a huge undertaking and one that may require changing some deeply ingrained habits. But there are some simple things you can do to control your chimp:

- Exercise your chimp. Find ways to consciously let it out of the cage on occasion, particularly before a situation where you think it might be a problem. You can't get rid of it, so let it say what it wants, then apply your human brain to the problem or situation. You might do this with some internal reflection or physical activity.

- Count to ten. It sounds simple, but a lot can be calmed down in ten seconds.

- Prepare for a situation you have coming up, where you know the chimp is likely to come out, by thinking about some coping mechanisms you can use to control the chimp when it does appear.

- Discuss controlling your chimps as a team. Come up with ways that work for you that would manage your collective chimps. Use language such as, 'Your chimp came out in that meeting yesterday'. This could help people understand when their chimp is triggered and how to deal with it. Great teams give permission to their team members to give constructive feedback to each other. Not just from the leader down, but peer-to-peer and from subordinate to leader, too.

- Read *The Chimp Paradox*. Like Jane, the more you understand about your chimp, the better you will be able to control it.

A word of warning – don't use the chimp to excuse bad behaviour. It is not OK to say, 'Well I'm not going to apologise for shouting at so-and-so – it was my chimp'. No. Ultimately, you are accountable for your actions, whether it was you doing it or your chimp. There's no excuse for inappropriate deployment of the chimp, letting him out deliberately, or passing the buck and blaming the chimp. Ultimately the 'chimp' is *you*.

How you like to communicate

Who we are as people is decided by a mix of nature and nurture. Some of who we are comes from our DNA, some from the way we were brought up, the culture we live in, our religion and other environmental factors. As much as we are all unique, with our own interplay of genes and environmental factors affecting our development, there are some commonalities that you will fit into. One thing is certain: your personality is a strong driver for how you prefer to communicate and handle the conflict necessary for your team to do well.

There are plenty of personality-profiling programmes out there, which are worth considering for what you can learn about yourself. There are some common learnings that come out of all of them.

Similarities and differences

One of the key learnings from personality-profiling tools is that you are going to be like some people and different from others. It sounds obvious, but I think we forget this easily in the heat of the moment. You will feel more comfortable communicating with people of a similar type to you and clash against people who are different. As soon as you accept this, you can start to switch from clashing to understanding, which is a vital lesson to take from the profiling process.

115

Balance

As we discussed earlier, it's important that teams have a good balance of all of personality types. If you were all one type, you would miss out on the good points of other personalities and you would all be guilty of the failings of your personality, too. There is no right or wrong when it comes to personalities – it is what it is, and that's all. You cannot judge someone for being the way they are. They didn't choose their strengths and weaknesses – it's just the way they were made.

Hold on, though. Before you start firing or hiring to attempt to create balance, all the traits will exist somewhere in your team and yourself, you just have to give voice to them. I have worked with some teams where there's a high percentage of one type of person in the room. For example, a construction company senior management team had a high percentage of task-focused, practical, competitive and blunt people, whereas a primary school faculty had a number of quieter, more empathetic and less forceful people. It's vital to remember that there's good in all the types. Your job as a team is to allow the good points to have expression to mitigate the bad.

The need for respect

You have to respect the different personality types to be able to encourage the better sides of them to come out. A key skill on great teams is a high 'EQ' – emotional intelligence – that is, the ability to empathise with others. When it comes to personality-driven communication, you have to put yourself in others' shoes and understand that they have different motivations and preferences from yours. It's not wrong, it's just different and we are all allowed to be that way.

Meeting in the middle

If you respect each other's preferences, then you should be willing to make some sacrifices of your own agenda, come out of your comfort zone and meet your teammates in the middle.

To get the best out of your interactions with others, make communication comfortable for all. Create an environment where discussions can be stress-free, where people feel able to express themselves, and you'll get the best out of people. Sometimes this means you coming out of your corner and being like someone else, temporarily overriding your natural preferences and consciously working in a different, perhaps uncomfortable way.

Bad communication

I have been present when communication goes horribly wrong. It can be toxic, with disastrous results for all involved. This is why getting your communication right is such a fundamental feature of great teamwork.

So much stems from there – the ability to make the right decisions, do great work, and even avoid damage to you and your team's physical health. It's that serious.

We can probably all remember times when our communication has been woeful. Times when we've been driven by our chimp, raised our voice or switched off. Bad communication can be passive as well as active, don't forget.

John Gottman is a professor of psychology and head of the Gottman Institute which specialises in couples therapy. He is also the author of *The Seven Principles for Making Marriage Work*. I choose to mention Gottman for a couple of reasons. First, he has comprehensive data gathered from monitoring couples over more than sixteen years, in what he calls the 'love lab' at the University of Washington in Seattle. This data enables him to predict with 91% accuracy whether a couple will divorce, based upon observing how they interact and communicate with each other. Second, he makes it easy to understand the key communication issues that will derail any relationship and, therefore, any team.[36]

Gottman identifies four key negative communication behaviours that are, in his words, 'so lethal to a

---

36   John Gottman, *The Seven Principles for Making Marriage Work*, p2.

relationship' that he calls them 'the Four Horsemen of the Apocalypse.'[37] These are:

- Criticism
- Defensiveness
- Stonewalling
- Contempt

When one or all of the above are present, then your communication is toxic. Contempt in particular is extremely damaging, to the point of being detrimental to your physical health.

The table below gives examples of what each of the four horsemen looks like.

	Characteristics
Criticism	Attacking, blaming, bullying, dominating, disrespecting, chronic complaining
Defensiveness	Looking for excuses, not taking the other person seriously, deflecting blame, not being open to influence
Stonewalling	Withdrawing from the interaction, turning away, refusing to engage, avoiding, being passive and withholding information
Contempt	Cutting others down, hostile gossiping, undermining, disrespecting, demeaning, mocking, being sarcastic, ridiculing, name-calling, eye-rolling, mimicking

---

37   John Gottman, *The Seven Principles for Making Marriage Work*, p32.

There are plenty of other bad behaviours, but for me, these are a good benchmark for when things are going wrong. We've all been guilty of them at some point. Maybe you are remembering right now when you have seen them at work – either from you, or from the people around you in your teams – including your marriage or other relationships.

It doesn't feel good, does it? In fact, it feels pretty terrible to know that we are capable of this kind of behaviour. But the good thing is, awareness of these 'four horsemen' is half the battle. Once you can actually personify them, put words to them and understand that they exist, then you can start to recognise when they are present and do something about them.

There is the potential within teams to have a perfect storm, where chimps are allowed to run free, where there is a lack of empathy for different personality types and Gottman's four horsemen are riding rough-shod through the team. This will not only create a toxic and stressful environment but will also ensure that the team has difficulty getting anything done.

How to communicate well

We now know more about some of the drivers of how we communicate – our inner chimp, our personality, our preferences – and how we get it wrong. Here are

some ways you can work towards getting communication right in your team.

Know how good your team is at communicating right now

When considering how you can become great at teamwork, do some honest reflection. Before you start to
make any changes, it's vital that you are aware of what
your faults are and what you are good at already. Here
are a few ways to get to know where your team is on
the scale of good or bad communication:

- Read widely on the subject – see the bibliography
  of this book for some suggestions.

- Hold an honest and open forum with your whole
  team to discuss communication. You'll need to
  warn everyone what the topic of the meeting is
  so they can prepare, but you should say from the
  outset that candid, honest and open conversation
  is going to be necessary. You can ask someone
  outside the team to facilitate it, if you think it will
  be a bit tricky to manage the discussion on your
  own.

- Undertake an assessment. Find one that works
  for you, fits with your budget, spare time and
  location, and with your team.

- Have one-to-one sessions with each team
  member, in which communication is the topic of

conversation. Giving feedback on each individual within the team privately will be especially beneficial if a particular individual needs to improve on the way they communicate, as you can say things you wouldn't in front of others.

- Consider engaging a team coach or communication expert who can come in for training to help your team discover its communication status. I am a big believer in engaging experts and paying for their services, as long as they are the right person to help your particular team and circumstance. You should ask yourself how much the direct cost will be now, versus the indirect cost that will occur over time if you don't get your communication right.

Involve everyone on the team

It's good if you are enthusiastically making personal changes in how you communicate because you want the team to be better. But you will have a greater chance of improving the whole team if all members work on their own communication skills. Get everyone involved and committed to change as much as you can. Share information. Perhaps hold discussion and discovery sessions to raise awareness. If you are the leader, you could go as far as making it a job requirement that your team members are expected to do this as part of their role.

A word of warning. Try not to be hesitant If the thought of broaching this topic with your team scares you or you fear people leaving because they don't want to change. As I've said before, great teamwork means having the right people on the team who fit with your culture and behavioural expectations. It means having tough conversations, making brave decisions and taking risks. If, like me, you believe that there's a right and wrong way to communicate in teams, and they are not going to change to the right way, then you have to seriously consider losing that person – either by their choice, or your instruction.

As leader, if you are serious about getting your team working right, you need to remove roadblocks. If that means people, then you should consider removing them from the team to make the right decision for the greater good. As Russell Lewis, author of *Company Commander* says, 'the popular decision will be right some of the time, the right decision will be right all of the time.'[38]

Banish the four horsemen

The four horsemen of toxic communication are dangerous bedfellows for every team and need to be banished. There is nothing positive about these behaviours. Even when debate and conflict are necessary to the team's communication, they need to be managed

---

38 Russell Lewis, *Company Commander*, p382.

respectfully. You cannot let these four riders into your team under any circumstances.

You need to work out how your team decides to not allow the horsemen in and how they stamp them out if they do arrive. It's difficult to offer concrete advice, as this can be a delicate subject and is influenced by factors that are particular to your team. But you must work out a way of banishing them. You could, for example, empower people to call each other out when they see them happening. I have heard of teams that have a 'red card' system, where everyone has a red card that they can hold it up if they see one of the four horsemen at work. You have to be careful with that policy – everyone needs to buy into that in advance – because the red card will be produced when emotions are running high.

There's something you need to be aware of about the four horsemen though. You may need to listen to the content of what the person is saying, even if they are saying it unskilfully. It may be something valuable that the team needs to hear. It is just being presented to the team in the wrong way. Often, we marginalise or ignore the dissenting voice, and try to shut it down because we don't like *how* it is speaking. Be careful not to ignore *what* is being said.

Work with the person to get them to deliver the information calmly and respectfully, without the presence of a horseman, so they can get their information heard. There is some percentage of truth in everything that is said within your team. The message may be difficult to hear, but don't dismiss it completely. Look for the real 'why' behind any voice that is speaking, no matter how awkwardly that voice is communicating. There may be some really necessary information trying to emerge.

Control your chimps

It's good advice for anyone in all walks of life to control their inner chimps, but it is especially important for the people you work or live with. Chimps on the rampage can do long-lasting damage. Trust takes a long time to build and a moment to break. An angry chimp could ruin a relationship if let loose at the wrong time. As we have learnt, working to ensure that each person on the team is able to control their chimp will improve your team's communication, no doubt about it.

Be better listeners

A lack of effective listening is one of the biggest failings of any team. Many of us find it hard to actively listen to people. It is important to listen for several reasons: to show respect, to get good ideas out of people, to allow people to share their opinion so they will buy into team decisions and to prevent misunderstanding and errors.

Active listening means two things. First, it means actually *listening*, if that makes sense – I mean allowing the speaker a voice, and you as the listener keeping quiet. It also means paying attention, focusing only on what the other person is saying and proactively processing their words. It means not doing something else at the same time, because we can only focus on one thing at a time. The fewer things anyone has to concentrate on, the better.

Put your phone down, turn towards the person talking, look into their eyes and be conscious and focused on what they are saying. Show them you are listening by nodding in agreement or asking qualifying questions to improve your understanding of what they are saying.

The importance of equality in listening and talking

I mentioned Sandy Pentland and his 'sociometric badge' previously and how he identified the concept of a 'charismatic connector'. Pentland's research has also emphasised the importance of creating a balance between time spent talking and listening across the team.

The research identifies five key conditions for creating equality of communication. These are:

1. Everyone on the team talks and listens in roughly equal measure, keeping contributions short and to the point.

2. Members face one another and their conversations and gestures are energetic.

3. Members connect directly with one another – not just with the team leader.

4. Members carry on back-channel or side conversations within the team.

5. Members periodically break, go exploring outside the team, and bring information back.

In addition to the above, Pentland's team discovered the three 'E's – three key factors for great communication on high-performing teams:

- Energy

- Engagement

- Exploration

Energy

Pentland's team defined energy as the amount of interaction that was going on. A nod, a gesture, a simple 'yes', as well as emails and text messages. They proved that face-to-face interaction is definitely the most productive type, followed by phone or video conferencing, although they also say that these are increasingly less effective the more people that join the conversation.

Engagement

Engagement reflects the distribution of energy among team members. If there's lots of energy being equally shared by all team members, then the engagement is strong. As soon as you start having imbalances with some people being more energetic than others, the engagement goes down. Think about it. On a team where people are not contributing and more importantly, not even moving – nodding in agreement, or similar – then you can tell they are not engaged. Teams where everyone is involved, contributing and sharing frequent energy are bound to be more engaged, which is a predictor of high-performance teamwork.

Exploration

Exploration describes the communication that team members enter into outside the confines of their own team. Pentland's research found a correlation between the amount of energy and connections teams had with other teams and high performance, especially when creativity and innovation were the performance indicators.

Teams of course need to balance the energy within and outside themselves. Communicative energy is important, but you also have to decide where and when it is focused. At times, you will need it to remain internal, whereas at other times, it will need to be externally focused. Energy can ebb and flow as time goes by and needs change, as long as there's balance and equality in its engagement.

It's amazing how accurate Pentland's findings are, and how they can inform advice or interventions which prove to be highly successful. They have 'been able to foretell, for example, which teams will win a business plan contest solely on the basis of data collected from team members wearing badges at a cocktail reception.'[39] In another example, call centre operatives for a bank were monitored, and one simple recommendation made – to synchronise the coffee breaks for teams within the call centre. This simple act saw profits increase by 15 million dollars and employee engagement scores go up 10%.

Regulating communication in meetings

Liz Wiseman in her book *Multipliers* talks about how she advised a leader who dominated discussions to play a game with poker chips. She gave him five chips to take into a meeting, with each one having a value in terms of seconds. One represented 120 seconds, three represented ninety seconds, and one represented thirty seconds. The leader was only allowed to speak for these durations and was only allowed to 'play'

39   Alex 'Sandy' Pentland, 'The new science of building great teams'.

the chips once in the meeting. He did so, with two interesting outcomes – he created the space necessary for others to speak, and he raised his credibility as a leader.[40]

You could create a similar concept within your team for meetings. Give everyone several chips to play. You can decide how many and the time value they represent. The people who usually dominate will have to choose their words carefully and speak less, while the people who normally don't speak up have to contribute more. You needn't even hand out actual chips – you could simply use the analogy to figure out who is doing all the talking or not, and use it as slang in your team vocabulary: 'John, you've used up all your chips,' or 'Valarie, you've not said anything, it's time you spent one of your chips,' and so on.

Fill the void – frequent communication

When I used to play rugby, we would discuss in training the level of talking that went on within the team, especially during a period of defensive activity when the opposition had the ball. Quiet defensive lines were weak. Keeping up a steady flow of chatter – and often this was shouted, constantly repeated words – worked. You had to keep telling your teammates where you were, who you were covering in the opposite team, what you could see that they couldn't,

---

40 Liz Wiseman, *Multipliers*, p91.

and what you were able to do or not do, so they could adjust and work with you to cover the pitch and prevent the opposition from scoring.

I remember coming off pitches almost hoarse because we'd all have been talking most of the time. This was a successful tactic, because it filled a void. When you are playing rugby or a similarly fast-paced team sport on a big pitch, you can only see and gather a certain amount of information. You also get tunnel vision, especially when you are in possession of the ball, and you rely completely on the other eyes and ears on your team to help you fill in the bigger picture of what's going on around you and elsewhere on the pitch. You need to know the things you can't see – for example, if a teammate is right beside you but just out of your peripheral vision, so you can pass the ball knowing that he will catch it. After all, you need to look out for your own safety, to keep checking where the opposition tacklers are. This is important when they are six-foot, 200-pound speedsters who are hell-bent on doing as much legal damage to you as they can.

Voids are gaps in your knowledge and understanding that are chinks in your armour as a team. On the rugby pitch, the opposition has a clear advantage if they can see a void and are able to fill it before your team does. Whatever your team is doing, you need to maintain frequent communication across your team in every direction, to fill any gaps and create clarity.

Ensuring everyone is clear on what's expected of them, where the support is and that they have all the information necessary to make decisions or achieve goals is all part of filling the voids. Just keep those lines of communication flowing.

Stay CALM

Team interactions can get incredibly heated. It's important that people remain cool, in order to make the most of the communication that is happening. Things can get very quickly out of control if people don't manage themselves. When emotions start to run high, the chimps start rattling the doors of their cages and we need to make sure we don't let them out. Remaining 'CALM' is a great piece of advice for difficult communication situations. This acronym stands for:

- Controlled – Stay in control of your emotions and words

- Adult – Be in an adult state of mind, not childish or letting your chimp out

- Listen – Stop and listen before you speak

- Measured – Keep your tone of voice measured and don't shout

SEVEN

Leadership

This couldn't be a book on teamwork if we didn't talk about leadership. Leadership and teamwork go hand in hand. You can't have one without the other. They are intrinsically linked and any team that aspires to become great absolutely has to have great leadership. Leadership done well is a strong predictor of a team's success, while leadership done badly is a sure-fire indicator of failure.

I don't lead – can I skip this chapter?

Before I go any further, if you are saying to yourself, 'I am not a leader, so I don't need to read this bit,' think again. Leadership is a behaviour across your team and is as much your responsibility as it is the actual person sitting in the leader's chair. You owe it to yourself and the whole team to take an interest. Yes, the actual leader influences you and the potential success of your team but the teammates under them each have a stake in leadership and can undertake their own leadership from their position in the team.

The landscape of leadership is changing as rapidly as it is for teams in general. One day you may well become a leader yourself, so why not get a head start on understanding it? Once you know more about how good leadership can be, if your leader isn't living up to standard, maybe you'll be better equipped to do something about it.

The new covenant of leadership

General Stanley McChrystal's book *Team of Teams* documents the commander's experiences of having to completely reorganise the structure and behaviours of the US military in response to an enemy and battlefield that was completely different to what they had seen before – that of Al Qaeda and the Taliban in Iraq and Afghanistan respectively. The US military had been designed to fight a conventional enemy and war, based upon a history that included two world wars, where the enemy operated in organised armies on designated battlegrounds and wore distinctive uniforms. You knew where the bad guys were, what they looked like and how to go after them.

Iraq and Afghanistan were completely different. These conflicts were closer in style to Vietnam, where the might of the American military had failed. The enemy lived among the civilian population, there was no clear territorial map, no 'us over here' and 'them over there'. McChrystal replaced all the maps, a key feature of any military operations room, with whiteboards and marker pens. This would be a war fought against a many-headed chimera of an enemy, based upon information rather than territory. Speed of response would be vital.

One of the things McChrystal writes about is how this required a completely different type of leader-ship than had gone before. He likened 'old' leader-ship to a game of chess – one commander dictating the moves of those around him. He called this 'heroic leadership', where the hero is expected to have all the answers, to lead the way and make all the decisions, and bask individually in the glory of victory.

This is very much how things had been done for cen-turies. Heroic leadership had worked in tandem with the hierarchical, highly structured organisations and cultures that dominated work, the military and other industries up until the new millennium.

McChrystal goes on to talk about the new kinds of leader in the modern world as 'gardeners' – since the act of 'nurturing the organization', as he puts it, is now vital to its success, which is a collective endeavour. The team's subordinates as well as its leader play a crucial part in their overall achievement. A good leader now does not dominate their team but affords their team members the freedom to make their own strategic moves while keeping an encouraging watch over them.[41]

The new covenant that leaders have with their people is one of empowerment, equality and encouragement. Leaders should no longer expect to be the ones in the limelight. Yes, they are still in charge and are ultimately responsible for the team's actions, but that's why they get paid more. But they don't get paid to have all the answers. Your team is going to be far more likely to succeed if you allow the people in it a voice.

Don't fall into the leadership trap of going backwards to the old 'top down' approach. Don't be a dinosaur. Embrace this new world order, if you want to optimise your chances of success. And don't forget that how you as a leader will be judged and measured is no longer based on your own merit, but on the success of the team around you. Share the podium with the empowered men and women who are as responsible for their team's glory as you are.

Egalitarian leadership

The new leadership model is flatter than the previous hierarchical structure. Previously, leaders were

---

41   Stanley McChrystal et al, *Team of Teams*, pp225, 231.

separated from the rest in so many ways. My father spent his career working for British Airways (formerly BOAC) and he remembers the days that the pilots, as the leaders on the plane, were treated differently from the rest of the team, the cabin crew. Pilots were addressed as 'sir', were never questioned, stayed in nicer hotels than the crew, and were transported to and from the plane in separate vehicles. They were a different class.

These old-style leaders were never challenged on their decisions and there were strict reporting lines. Leadership is now a more egalitarian affair, in keeping with the principle that all people are equal and deserve equal rights and opportunities. In the context of leadership, this for me means the idea that everyone on the team can have input into leadership at some point and in some way during their working life on the team. A leader should expect to be challenged by their team, and to pass the mantle of leadership over to others for specific tasks, for example, when another team member is better suited to making a particular decision than the de facto leader.

Leaders might feel nervous to embrace this style. To give responsibility to others to make decisions and do things that might fail, when their neck will ultimately be the one on the block if it goes wrong is a challenging concept. You need to take a leap of faith to make this move. But like jumping into a pond where you don't know how cold the water is, or how deep, it will all be OK once you jump in.

Stanley McChrystal went through this barrier in Iraq. He describes the process of decision-making and seeking permission to conduct an operation or fire a missile as torturously long, requiring going up a long chain of command and back down again to the operative on the ground. By the time permission was granted, the window of opportunity had closed. Al Qaeda would melt into the darkness before the missile could be engaged. He also found that people were waking him up in the middle of the night to ask, 'Sir, can we fire this missile?' only for him to think something along the lines of, 'Well, you tell me, you are the ones with all the facts at your fingertips – I don't know the situation.'

He couldn't of course say that, as he was the boss who had to give permission, but it made him think. What's the risk of us empowering these guys on the ground to make these decisions? He found that, in general, the risks of acting too slowly were higher than letting competent people make their own decisions, in summary, accepting 'the 70 percent solution today, rather than satisfying protocol and getting the 90 percent solution tomorrow'.[42]

---

42 Stanley McChrystal et al, *Team of Teams*, p209. McChrystal goes on to say, 'In the military you learn that you will never have time for the 100 percent solution.'

The point here is that they worked out the odds. What is holding them back from moving towards this more egalitarian model, where they are trusting junior people to make decisions that were previously the preserve of the senior leadership? The understandable fear that these people won't get it right. We will accept a greater margin of error, because it's worth it to capitalise on the time advantage it will give us.

I completely understand the reticence in leaders who are loath to trust their people to make bigger decisions or use their own initiative. You want to control your own destiny. You want to give your expertise and experience to the situation. But at what cost? Organisations today are always under pressure to make quick responses and empowering your team to make decisions removes the delay of seeking hierarchical approval. By including them, you are also tapping into their expertise.

What did McChrystal find when they introduced this initiative which he called 'empowered execution'? Surprisingly, he found that as authority was decentralised and delegated further down the chain, the quality of decisions made actually improved. So, in effect they were getting the 90 percent solution today, after all.[43]

The leap of faith paid off. Although it seemed counterintuitive to delegate more decisions to less experienced

---

43   Stanley McChrystal et al, *Team of Teams*, p214.

team members, they were getting better results than they expected. But this doesn't come without some teething problems and hard work to get it going. I don't think you can just say, 'OK guys, over to you to make the decisions – see you later'. You need to seed the ground and prepare your team for their new role. This includes creating a few ground rules and expectations of what is allowed and what isn't. You have to judge the readiness of your team and organisation to accept this mature and responsible way of doing things. McChrystal talks about creating a 'shared consciousness' upon which this decentralised decision-making can exist as a fundamental building block. As leader, you first need to draw up the plans to put that block in place.[44]

How do I lead in this modern world?

You might be asking 'What should we as leaders be doing differently, if we are going to give our team a shot at the dizzy heights of greatness?' I am reminded of an exercise called 'Stop, Start, Keep' that I have used when working with teams – what are we going to stop doing, start doing and keep doing? Some of the old ways are still valid and don't need to change. Some need to end, and some new ones need to be introduced.

---

44   See Chapter 10, 'Hands Off', of Stanley McChrystal's *Team of Teams* for more detail about this.

I am going to outline my key instructions for modern leadership. If you are a team leader, I hope you are already doing some or most of this, in which case this will be a validation exercise. If not, then maybe you can start to do more. If you are a team member, you can see what you should expect of your leader and do something about it if they aren't doing enough.

Empower your team to make decisions

As we've already seen, it's time to devolve decision-making to others. Don't do this without some ground rules but have faith that your team will be quicker at making decisions overall, and those who make decisions in this way will become more invested in the outcome.

Involve your team and keep them informed

Involve your team in what is going on. Keep people informed about the bigger picture, about future plans, what other teams are doing and why certain things are happening. This gives your team members a sense of worth and avoids them feeling disconnected or unengaged. Seek their opinion and ask for their ideas so they know that they matter. You should especially keep them tuned in to your team's goals and purpose.

Allow people to make mistakes

Mistakes are where learning and innovation happen. If people feel they cannot make a mistake, they will be frozen into inactivity, fearing the consequences of getting things wrong. It's far better that people feel able to take a risk or make a decision without worrying about the consequence. It's incredibly empowering for your team to know they are trusted. Demonstrating the trust you have in your people will allow them to repay their trust back to you.

Harness the hidden talents of your team

Liz Wiseman in her book *Multipliers* talks about the concept of 'native genius'[45] – the things that people are innately good at and passionate about, and that they will do willingly and freely for no additional pay, just because they love it so much. You'd be surprised at what native genius lies hidden within your team that you could unlock to your advantage. Mine for these gems of talent and exploit them, to everyone's advantage. Allowing that person to indulge in their passion and skill will keep them happy, loyal and engaged, and you might find a skill you can use for no extra cost.

---

45 Liz Wiseman, *Multipliers*, pp46–48.

Listen

A good leader does as much, if not more, listening than they do talking. Listening is one of the best tools in your leadership toolkit. Ask lots of open questions and try not to immediately lead with your opinion and a premeditated decision. By listening to your team, not only might you find a better course of action, but you are also ensuring better engagement and opportunities for commitment from the team than if you just talk at them. Listen actively. Give that person your undivided attention, look them in the eye, nod when they talk, don't fidget and, for goodness' sake, put your phone away.

Always listen to both sides of the argument

When someone comes to you with an issue, make sure you understand the other side of the coin before you act. It's easy to be swayed by one person's impression or opinion, especially if it sounds convincing, comes from someone you trust, or if you are tempted to accept their word because it's the easy route. But you have to make sure you've covered every angle so you can make a fair judgement and act with the confidence that you have covered every viewpoint. Don't assume anything and try to have as many of the facts at your disposal before jumping to conclusions.

Become a master of the art of the question

It is tempting for leaders to fall into the old trap of being the one with all the answers. Throw this idea out and replace it with being the one who has all the questions. The know-it-all leader should be consigned to the scrap heap of leadership history. Using questions is such a powerful weapon in your leadership arsenal. You can use questions to uncover the expertise of people around you. You will also get more buy-in from your team members if they commit to work that is asked of them, and that they contributed to by answering your questions, rather than if you just tell them what to do.

Stand up for your people

Sometimes it's your job to stand up for your people, even at the expense of your own position. It's that important. As a leader, you must be prepared to defend your team when necessary. Be principled, be honourable and take a stand.

Monitor the health of your team

Keep checking in on how your team are doing. If you have a team charter, check on it regularly. Are you connected to your purpose? How are you doing with your goals? How's the team – any issues, any problems?

Take the time to make sure there are no bumps in the road coming up that you could deal with now.

Be consistent

There's nothing worse than bosses who say one thing, then do another, or who don't fulfil their promises. Be consistent in how you act, how you ask people to behave and follow through on what you promise. This will build trust – that cornerstone of good teamwork.

Don't forget to offer praise

Don't underestimate how far a few words of praise, thanks and encouragement can go to securing greater loyalty, commitment and effort from your team. It will make you feel good, too, to see the smile on people's faces. And remember the maxim of 'Praise in public, reprimand in private' – people love to be praised within earshot of their peers and colleagues.

Be prepared to make unpopular decisions

Leadership is not a popularity contest. You will at times have to make a decision that won't go down well with those it impacts. Do you remember the difference between the right decision and the popular decision? The right decision is right all of the time, the popular decision is right some of the time. As a leader, it's guaranteed that at some point you will make decisions that people won't like. It comes with the job.

Get to know your team

One of the biggest signs of job misery is anonymity. Pat Lencioni highlights this as one of the three signs of a miserable job in his book *The Truth About Employee Engagement*.[46] You don't have to be everyone's friend – far from it – but it is absolutely your job to take a personal interest in the people you lead. Don't underestimate how important a few simple questions about someone's family, hobby or problem they are facing are. Showing a genuine interest in the answer is a given. Acting on what they say will win you followers rather than subordinates.

Walk the fine line between friend and boss

In the old model, there were formal lines between bosses and their team, with clear delineation of roles. Those days are gone. It's more productive now for leaders to strike up friendships with their team members. But once you become too close with someone, your authority could be compromised and your position undermined. You may need to discipline them someday or ask them to do something they don't

---

46   Pat Lencioni, *The Truth About Employee Engagement*.

want to do. It's a fine line, and the line is in different places for each person and situation. But walk on the right side of it – and don't cross it.

Find out what motivates your people

A boss of mine once asked me in our first meeting together, 'What motivates you?' Do you know what motivates each person you manage? Not everyone is motivated the same way. Don't assume that everyone is motivated by money. You'd be surprised what you find out, which you can then use to get the best out of people. Once you know what makes your team members tick, you can use this knowledge in a good way, to keep them happy, driven and productive.

Check in with your team frequently

Another tactic that should be consigned to the leadership scrap heap is the annual review. Let me rephrase that – it's OK to have an annual review, but not if that's the only time you check in with your people. You should be checking in frequently: weekly or fortnightly. You don't have to have a long formal meeting every week, but a five- to ten-minute chat to make sure they are OK and moving in the right direction. If you only ask three questions in the check-in, here are my best three: 'How are you?' 'What are you focusing on this week?' and 'How can I help you do what you need to do?'

When you need to give feedback, give it

So many leaders shy away from giving feedback, especially if it's going to be unpopular. It's tempting to hide behind emails or not give feedback at all. This is one of the areas where leaders earn the extra money and other perks they receive – by giving feedback when it needs to be given. And when you do give feedback...

Do feedback right

There are some basic principles to keep in mind when giving feedback. Whenever possible, do it in person, and do it often. Don't neglect giving people positive feedback. Sometimes bosses take for granted the good work being done around them, and only give negative or what should be called 'improvement feedback'. A pat on the back and a simple 'Well done' can go a long way. If you have to give improvement feedback, have all the facts prepared in advance. Think through how the conversation will go and plan how you will handle the person's response before you start. Don't let your emotions rule the conversation – remain calm. Listen to their side of the story. Conclude your meeting with a positive, forward-looking action plan.

Reinforce the context

I am constantly amazed when people panic and worry over the slightest thing. A classic and frequent example I have seen too often is people getting worked up because a delegate at an event didn't have a name badge. Really? It's a name badge. No one is losing an arm. OK, if you are in a war or an operating theatre it's a bit different, but most of us are lucky that we don't work in an environment where lives are on the line. What's the worst that is going to happen? Let's be realistic when people think they need to panic or get worked up – your job as a leader is to rein things in and put them into the appropriate context.

Be the CRO

Every leader needs to make sure that the team knows why they are doing what they are doing. Seek every opportunity you can to be the CRO – the Chief Reminding Officer – to remind people why you are asking them to do what they are doing. Make sure they are connected to the purpose of why your team exists and what it is there to achieve. You cannot do this often enough. Repeat, reinforce, *remind*.

Stay calm and don't radiate panic

Major Russell Lewis MC wrote a book about his experience of leading troops in battle during his tour of duty in Afghanistan with the British Army's Parachute Regiment in 2008, titled *Company Commander*. As a young officer, he had been given some great advice from his commanding officer that stuck with him throughout his military career, which was: 'Stay cool on the net.'

The net is short for the radio network. He explained that when you, the commander, speak on the radio, everyone can hear you. They are listening not only to your words, but also to your emotion. They will read as much in to *how* you are saying something as to what you are saying. If you panic, they will panic. If you are calm and measured, they will stay calm and measured. Before you speak on the radio, take a second, think through what you want to say and then be 'cool on the net'.[47]

If you haven't managed to keep things in context (and don't worry – it happens – we are human, after all) and you are panicking, don't show it. Your mood as the leader is highly infectious and people are watching you for guidance, especially if the pressure is on. Don't run – literally and figuratively speaking – and portray an outer image of calm, even if your feelings are bubbling like mad under the surface. If you panic, your people will jump on that roller coaster with you.

---

47   Russell Lewis, *Company Commander*, p7.

Be supportive of the good people who leave your team

It's a sad day when a good person leaves your team. If you have explored why they want to go and there's nothing you can do to keep them, don't resist. Support their future and wish them well. Be thankful for the contribution they made and keep them in your network – you never know what they will go on to do. People are moving jobs with increasing frequency in the modern world of work, so you can't prevent it in many cases. It's best to go with it than fight against it.

Treat others how you would like to be treated

This is the golden rule. It's a fundamental value common to every major religion the world has ever seen. It's so simple, but so effective. At the end of the day, if you remember nothing else about leadership, always treat others as you would like to be treated yourself.

EIGHT
Ready To Launch

The romance of space travel excites and inspires humankind. 650 million people watched as Neil Armstrong took those first immortal steps on the surface of the moon. 'One small step for man, one giant leap for mankind.' Epic stuff.

Think for a minute about the moment of launch. The astronaut is being strapped into his seat, the fuel is being poured into the immense rocket and the door is being closed. Mission Control is counting down. 'Five minutes and counting...' Imagine the pressure. When Alan Shepherd was sitting in this seat on the 1961 Mercury mission, about to be the first American launched into space, his heart was beating at around 200 beats per minute.

Every team has a launch point. All the planning has been done, the team selected, the rocket fuelled. A clear purpose and goals have been identified and selected. It's time to start walking the walk. The journey is about to begin.

The first cut is the deepest

In 1967, PP Arnold released the popular song, 'The First Cut is the Deepest'. It's a classic, covered by artists up to and including Sheryl Crow's version in 2005. Why do I mention it here? Because the first minutes, seconds even, of your team's existence and interaction together are the most important. I would hope that there are no cuts, but you can make the deepest, longest-lasting impressions with that first gathering of people, when they start to work as a team.

Teams all need some sort of kicking off, a launch point. Work will have been done beforehand to put the team together in the first place. But at some point, the countdown clock reaches zero and it's time for the off – time to do whatever it is you are there to do.

Imagine that your team at this point is a blank canvas, or a book full of blank pages, ready to record your journey. As soon as the first mouth is opened and the first words come out, the pen goes to the paper, and records what is happening. You immediately define this team by its words and actions. You cannot rub out the picture that is being painted, or the words that are being recorded. They will forever stand as a record of your team's existence and they will influence everything that happens next.

The first seconds and minutes of your team's existence are vital. Your ability to positively influence the team's culture, beliefs, what it stands for, how it will work, what it will do, is at its peak in those first few moments. Once things start happening, it is impossible to undo them. Make the first interaction count.

Too many teams neglect to start their life with some time focused on how they are going to work together. It's all too easy, especially in the world today, where time is the resource we often have in shortest supply, to just get on with the job at hand. This is the same whether your team's lifespan is just a day or years in place. There are few teams who take the time to stop and proactively work on their teamwork in the first few moments of their existence.

In an interview with *Harvard Business Review*, J Richard Hackman identified that people often fail to realise that the first few minutes at the start of the life of a team are critical; they can establish the direction of the group, its relationship with its leader and the norms to which the team will be expected to conform.

Hackman described a conversation he had with Christopher Hogwood, the distinguished conductor of the

Handel and Haydn Society in Boston. They talked about how important the first rehearsal would be, when he first stood up as the guest conductor of a new orchestra: 'What do you mean, the first rehearsal?' he asked. 'All I have is the first few minutes.' He went on to explain that there's nothing he pays greater attention to than the way he starts the first rehearsal.[48]

To not spend even a few minutes focusing time and effort on moulding your team is to potentially set yourself up for failure from the start. If you don't spend this early time on your team, you are leaving a lot up to chance. Team cultures and accepted behaviours will be decided by default, often under the influence of the most dominant or vocal members of the group, who aren't always the best people to be guided by.

I also know that many leaders and teams don't know the recipe for great teamwork. I have worked with so many teams who don't understand the importance of learning about the skills of successful teamwork, or who have never been taught proper teamwork. There's often lots of highly intelligent, highly trained people, many of whom have had large amounts of money spent on developing their job or leadership skills, but they fall into the same trap that most teams

48   Diane Coutu, 'Why teams don't work: An interview with J Richard Hackman', *Harvard Business Review*, 2009, https://hbr.org/2009/05/why-teams-dont-work, accessed 28 February 2020.

do – they get stuck into the task at hand before they've agreed some vital, but undervalued, stuff up front.

If your team is already in existence and down the track, don't feel it's too late to bother with this. It's never too late to start taking care of your team and consciously working on how you are going to succeed together. You can still do the things I am suggesting for a new team. It is never a waste of time.

The team charter

Humans have evolved into a species that lives and works relatively harmoniously in tribal societies alongside fellow human beings. We wouldn't have survived without some guiding principles that were developed and handed down from generation to generation, which govern how we behave and the morals we agree to. From the earliest religious texts to the modern-day constitutions of nations, we have created these documents, these instructions books and even commandments that guide our society, our tribe, or team, in how we act every day.

Your team needs its own version of this, its own constitution. It needs a charter, a set of principles and rules that will inform all the people on your team what it is that the team is doing, how everyone on it is expected to behave, and what you stand for.

Before you think, 'Oh no, we really don't have time to go through the process of coming up with a team charter,' I hear you. Teams these days are often formed quickly and disband sometimes just as quickly. Their shelf life is short, and you don't need to go through a lengthy chartering process if this is the case. You can do a simple chartering process verbally in a couple of minutes to get basic agreement in place for how you are going to work together. On the other hand, if your team is going to be more complex, large, or have a long shelf life, you should spend more time creating this charter in detail.

Six questions to determine a team charter

What's this idea of a team charter all about, and what needs to go in it? First, the charter gives you an anchor point. Going back to the analogy of the book with the blank pages, the first thing you are going to write in it are the details of your team charter. This is the jumping off point for your team to go and do the work it has formed to do. But instead of leaving what you do to chance, you will be armed with the guidelines, playbook and information required to keep yourselves focused on the right course and behaving the right way.

All the work you will do is built upon the foundation of this charter. It is your purpose. Your goals. How you allow and expect people to behave. How you will make decisions. What you will do when you face obstacles in the road. You need to answer the six questions of team chartering, to give your team the focus it needs. The questions are as follows. (Here's a tip to help you remember them. I think of the six questions as five 'W's and one 'H' – or 6WH questions – why, who, what, when, where and how).

1. Why do we exist?

This is a simple check-in on what you should already have worked out, your overarching, compelling purpose – your reason for being. Hopefully you have managed to craft this into a phrase or sentence with meaning and impact, that people relate to and clearly understand, and which can be the first thing you ink into your charter.

2. Who does what?

Who is on your team and what do they do? This question simply identifies whom the charter applies to and their role in the team. Who is the leader? Who can I go to if I need something? Some clear information about who does what is important to confirm from the start.

3. What do we need to do?

What are the goals we have that will tell us when we are being successful? Remind yourselves of these. If you haven't already identified them, now is the time to do so. Check back in on the previous chapter on goals to work this bit out. If you are creating a physical document (more on that below) you may not have room for all your goals on that, so maybe pick your top three, or one key goal that everyone can relate to. This will give you some focus and remind you of the others you need to check in on.

4. When do we do it?

This question should cover two things: What's the lifetime of your team, and when do you physically work? Some teams are deadline-driven. Some work in a more open-ended way. For some teams, this will be more relevant but having a handle on your team's expected lifetime is important.

This question might spark some conversation about work–life balance. Do you allow people to be contacted at night, or expect them to be working unsociable hours? How do you govern the team if you work in different time zones? We are asking some big questions about how we work together in terms of physical space and time, and people often have radically different expectations of when we work. Some companies allow flexible working. This needs to be clarified and a ruling made from the start about when people are expected to be working.

5. Where do we work?

Physical space should be considered, not only in terms of where on the playing field, in the town, country or world we do what we do, but also physically where the team members are expected to physically work? Take the example of a football team. It's obvious that the players will work on the pitch during the game, but you might decide to introduce rules about where on the pitch each player is expected to work? Defenders near the goal, attackers up front. Are office workers expected to physically be in the office? What about field sales teams? Where do they operate?

The COVID-19 pandemic has radically changed where people work, with many workers forced to work from home in isolation during lockdown. Teams have had to quickly adapt to this way of working, with online video conferencing taking the place of face-to-face interactions. At the time of writing this is still the case, and it will be interesting to see how much of an effect this will have on where teams work. Many teams won't return to working the same way they did before the pandemic, and with increased remote working, organisations will need to agree up front the rules about where people can work.

6. How do we work?

This question is potentially the biggest one to answer, and arguably the most important at this stage of the process. Where and when should be easy to establish, and you should already know the answer to the why, who and what you do. But how? It's a big question, covering a lot of angles, all of which are important. Mostly it looks at how you are going to behave as a team. What is allowed, and what isn't?

Mario Moussa, Madeline Boyer and Derek Newberry in their book *Committed Teams* talk about covering these norms of behaviour at the outset and recommend looking at three basic teamwork activities, at least agreeing on how you will handle three of the most important team activities, and the ones most prone to causing problems. They identify these as:

- How do we resolve conflicts?

- How do we communicate?

- How do we make decisions?[49]

Establishing agreed ground rules with the team about how to do these things at the very least are important. If you can't communicate effectively, resolve conflicts when they arise and make good, timely decisions, your team is going to struggle.

You need to manage this section of your charter carefully. Part of me loves the simplicity of the New Zealand All Blacks approach – just saying 'No dickheads'

49   Mario Moussa, Madeline Boyer and Derek Newberry, *Committed Teams*, p15.

works on many levels. Everyone pretty much knows when someone is behaving like a dickhead. But it is important that you cover these three basics as a minimum and work up some guidelines. Be aware that they may open up more questions and possibilities, based upon the different scenarios you see coming your way.

How to manage the chartering phase

Managing the process of completing and agreeing on your charter is vital. Remember that the first moments of your existence hugely influence the rest of your time together, so you must get them right. If you are not careful, you could end up having a complete free-for-all with no charter and a lot of conflict as a result – just what you don't need. To avoid this, here are some tips on how to carry out the chartering process.

Get everyone together for a chartering session

I advise you do everything you can to get everyone in the room together to take part in crafting your team's charter. I appreciate that in today's global economy, with many teams spread over all continents, this may not be practical, but I recommend you do what you can to make it happen. There's power in having everyone physically together to contribute ideas, debate points and ultimately agree and buy into the validity of the charter. You will have a better chance of creating the commitment necessary for you to hold people accountable if you draw the charter up in person. If you can't get your team in the same room, the next best thing would be a video conference call.

To create a physical charter – or not?

Do you need an actual physical document where you record this? Yes and no, depending on your circumstances. If you are a quick project team that has a simple job and you won't be together long, you probably don't need one. Maybe you can have a playing card-sized prompter you keep in your wallet or handbag. Maybe you are all used to the concept of this chartering process from previous projects you have worked on, and you know a lot of the 'how' stuff has already been covered. Everyone is familiar with behavioural expectations and you just need a quick five minutes to go over the six chartering questions verbally, more for a reminder and affirmation than anything else. Spending time populating a document would be wasteful, in this instance.

On the other hand, if you are a brand new team with lots of people who don't know each other and who aren't used to the chartering process, you may like to spend more time on this, creating a physical document you can keep and refer to over time. This will also help you hold people accountable and remind them what's expected – this is useful when you are deep into your journey and the heat is on. We've already talked about the concept of being the Chief

Reminding Officer and how you need to focus things when your team is in the troughs of its existence. A physical charter is a great tool to be able to pull out and look at when the going gets tough.

Allow the right amount of time for the process

This goes hand in hand with the need (or not) for a physical charter. You could spend five minutes going over the six chartering questions, or at least just the relevant ones you need to cover, in a stand-up, kick-off meeting. This would especially be the case for an organisation that is well practised in the art of agile teamwork, forming and disbanding teams quickly to answer particular needs or solve sudden problems. Think of an American Football team, when the offence forms a huddle to take five seconds to agree the next play – this is a form of chartering.

For larger, more complex or settled teams, you should allow more time. You might even take a whole day or longer off-site to do it. In my experience, the bigger the reason for being, the longer your team will be together, the more complex the issues involved, the more time you will need to plan. Only you can decide exactly how long you'll need. But take this seriously, and don't try to create a complex charter that answers a lot of questions in ten minutes. Going off with a half-baked outline is almost as dangerous as not drawing one up at all.

Seek external help

It is a good idea to seek the services of someone outside your team to help you through this process. They will give you an impartial view and different perspective. Having someone facilitate the process will help you manage it, keep you on time and leave no stone unturned. It might cost you some money if you hire a facilitator or coach, but a little bit of time and money spent now could prevent a higher cost further down the road if things start to go wrong.

Make it look nice

If you decide to create a physical charter, then make it look attractive. We respond to colour and images and an attractive-looking charter could bring it to life. You could go as far as getting a graphic designer to create a wonderful charter that you would be proud to hang on the wall.

Get the team to sign the charter

If you have completed a physical charter, and you have made it colourful and easy to understand, then get all the people who are governed by it to sign it. We've used signatures since we first invented language to secure commitment and hold people accountable. There is still power in making our mark on a document to signify our commitment towards what that document covers – contracts, mortgages, marriage certificates – signatures still have validity, even in the digital age.

Keep your charter alive

Once you have completed your charter, don't just file it away to gather dust in a drawer. It is a living part of your team. Make it visible and revisit it frequently. Parts of it will potentially change over time. You are unlikely to have got it 100% right on the first pass, and things will happen that you have not foreseen which you need to adjust for. Bring it out at meetings, put it on the wall, send it to the team by email, create smaller pocket-sized versions or desktop versions... be as creative as you can in making this an integral part of your team's journey. See it and live it every day.

If/then thinking

The authors of *Committed Teams* say, 'If/then thinking deals with a potential problem by identifying what you will do if you encounter it. This is one of the defining characteristics of people who are consistently able to attain their goals.'[50] They go on to describe how if/then thinking is one of the key attributes of people who consistently achieve their goals.

---

50   Mario Moussa et al, *Committed Teams*, p9.

The concept of a pre- rather than a post-mortem can be powerful. Just before a downhill skier enters the hut where they will start their run, they stand there, eyes closed, hand raised out in front of them with their palm flat and facing downwards, mimicking themselves and imagining their impending progress down the hill. They project themselves mentally onto the slope, and imagine every turn, every jump, and how they are going to act when they get there, moving their hand up and down, side to side, as if their hand is them ski-ing. They go through the route in their head, anticipating in advance what is going to happen, so they are ready in case there's a problem.

This visualisation method is a great way of imagining what it's going to be like as you progress through your journey and can be applied to your team as well. This is about anticipating potential pitfalls, threats or any issues that could derail your team and disrupt your progress. That's the 'if'. Next you come up with a 'then' response. If x happens, then we will do y.

You must judge how far you go with this. You can't spend days thinking through every tiny thing that could go wrong. You have to judge how much time it is worth spending on this. Teams that work in risky environments, where lives are on the line, are already practised at this. For example, the military do this, with their 'Actions on' mentality. What actions do we take on capture? What actions do we take on closing with the enemy? What actions do we take if our helicopter crashes behind enemy lines? Soldiers have a phrase which demonstrates the need for if/then thinking: 'No plan survives contact with the enemy.'

That you have even had a conversation around this kind of if/then thinking is a benefit. Training the mind to anticipate problems and how to deal with them will also help your reaction to the ones you haven't been able to anticipate. If, as a team, you are practised in this concept, it will stand you in good stead when the unexpected happens. Identifying obstacles and having responses in place will be tremendously beneficial to your team and will increase the chance of you being able to cope with them if they hit.

The checklist

Atul Gawande is a surgeon at Harvard Medical School and author of *The Checklist Manifesto*. The basic premise of the book is about the power of checklists to help reduce errors in the complex world of work that so many of us find ourselves in. The idea came about when Gawande and his team noticed that the error rate in surgery was unacceptably high and wanted to find ways to reduce it. Like all good teams do, they looked outside their immediate environment for answers, and one thing they noticed was how pilots run through a checklist before take-off. They thought maybe they could incorporate this idea into the way they work in operating theatres.

Gawande's team came up with a short list that addressed the major common problems faced in surgery. This was not an exhaustive list – it consisted of nineteen items, taking under two minutes to complete and was based around three common problems in theatre – those with anaesthesia, blood loss and team communication. One of the indicators of the checklist's success would be whether it would reduce deaths on the operating tables.

Apart from the obvious but necessary questions like, 'Does the patient have an allergy?' or 'Is the [surgical] site marked?' much of the list concerned team communication. Things like, 'Has everyone in the room introduced themselves by name and role?' 'Have they confirmed the patient's name, procedure and where the incision will be made?' 'Has the surgeon articulated key concerns for recovery and management of this patient?'

The checklist was introduced in eight hospitals across the world, in countries including the UK, Canada, Tanzania and India. In the period of study, they witnessed a 50% reduction in operating theatre deaths. The tactic proved to be so successful that the World Health Organization adopted it for use across the globe.

I love the simplicity and effectiveness of this idea – it's often the simple ones that have the biggest impact. It works well with a complex situation. There's obviously lots of moving parts in operating theatres and plenty that can go wrong. But you could employ a checklist for any action your team starts. If you want to do this, there are a few interesting things worth considering.

When to use a checklist

Primarily the checklist is something you'd use before you start some action or practice you are about to undertake. But Gawande's checklist has a section to be ticked off just before the patient leaves theatre at the end of the surgery. This was a key moment for the patient, where the surgical team could help to prevent issues arising once patients left theatre. If you want to introduce a checklist, think where it would be most appropriate, where the most errors occur that you could reduce.

Simplicity

Gawande's checklist is simple. Nineteen points that take two minutes to complete. A checklist shouldn't be any longer than that. It shouldn't become a burdensome practice that people won't adopt because it's too cumbersome and unwieldy to use.

The importance of teamwork

I am fascinated that Gawande's team worked out that one of the three major issues to address was not about what they did – performing surgery – but instead concerned team communication, a problem that afflicts every team to varying degrees. If you looked for error points within your team or teams, would you find that a significant proportion of them would be in how you work as a team, rather than the actual work you do? I'm willing to bet that a similar assessment of teams in all walks of life would give us similar results to Gawande.

Your attitude towards mistakes

One of the things great teams do is having the right attitude towards mistakes. Mistakes happen. They are a fact of life. But for some of us, the stakes are higher than for others. Gawande's team were working at a very high-stakes table – literally – where lives were on the line every day, so their attitude to risk and tolerance of mistakes is different from mine as I click-clack away at my keyboard. But whatever the stakes, being aware that errors happen is the important thing, and it can often be the stupidest, simplest things we get wrong.

How your team deals with mistakes is important. Liz Wiseman talks in her book *Multipliers* about Lutz Ziob, who took over as general manager of Microsoft's education business in 2003. Ziob allowed mistakes because he realised they were a necessary result of taking risks, which the company needed to take at that time. One of Ziob's managers, Chris Pirie, talked about his attitude, describing how he made mistakes but learnt fast. He failed on occasion, but he never made the same mistake twice.[51] Gawande's team was trying to stamp out mistakes, which were costly for them as well as their patients, who paid the ultimate price. But the point here is that you can decide how you'll deal with mistakes and should have a clear policy with your team that works for what you do.

Speaking up

One item on Gawande's checklist was to make sure everyone had introduced themselves by name. The effect of this was what Gawande refers to as the 'activation phenomenon'. Having had the chance to speak their name, Gawande's team members were more likely to speak up if problems occurred.

One of the issues with some surgical teams is the lofty position some surgeons hold over other staff, for example, the nurses in the operating theatre. We've heard the term 'God complex' applied to those surgeons who think so much of themselves, they create an environment around them where people are afraid to speak up and challenge their actions, even if they

---

51   Liz Wiseman, *Multipliers*, p86.

are doing something wrong. It is interesting that 20% of surgeons opposed the idea of the checklist when it was going to be introduced. To overcome this resistance, the surgeons were asked, 'If you were to have an operation, would you want a checklist?' 94% of them said they would.[52]

To return to the point about the activation phenomenon that occurred just by getting people to introduce themselves by name, we can see that it feeds into creating an atmosphere of psychological safety. If a junior theatre nurse dare not challenge a senior surgeon, the checklist question increases her feeling of being able to speak up. If you need to be really bullish about increasing psychological safety in your team, you could make it obvious by including on your team's checklist something like, 'Has the senior leader on the team given express permission to everyone to speak up?'

If/then thinking

Atul Gawande's checklist is also a great example of if/then thinking. The surgical team is preparing for eventualities as well as trying to iron out problems before they happen. Have we got enough blood in case we need to do a transfusion? Do we know if the patient has an allergy? Is essential imaging displayed?

---

52 'Atul Gawande's "Checklist" for surgery success', *NPR*, 2010, www.npr.org/templates/story/story.php?storyId=122226184, accessed 28 February 2020.

All these questions are designed to anticipate trouble and prepare a solution, if or when it happens. It's no surprise that there was such a great result when they introduced this tool.

Ready to launch

I wrote this book to help anyone who exists in a team. Most of us do, in some shape or form, and life in teams is not perfect. You now have some ideas, tips and tools that will help your team work more effectively together. Whatever walk of life that team is in, whether it's at work or at home, new or old, small or large, these things can work for you. Sometimes all it takes is a small course correction now to reach a better destination in the future.

I urge you to do what it takes for your team to have a better life. The rewards are worth it. If things are broken, they can be fixed. Be brave and take the first steps to fix the issues you can see in front of you, together as a team. I wish you the best of luck and good team health in the future.

Bibliography

Bohns, Vanessa K, 'A face-to-face request is 34 times more successful than an email', *Harvard Business Review*, 2017, https://hbr.org/2017/04/a-face-to-face-request-is-34-times-more-successful-than-an-email, accessed 28 February 2020.

Brewer, Geoffrey, 'Snakes top list of Americans' fears', *Gallup*, 2001, https://news.gallup.com/poll/1891/snakes-top-list-americans-fears.aspx, accessed 4 March 2020.

Cambridge University, 'Cambridge ideas – The Boat Race: A perfect crew?', 2009, www.youtube.com/watch?v=MXLg9nsuo9I, accessed 28 February 2020.

Challen, Paul, *The House that Hugh Laurie Built*, 2007, ECW Press, Toronto.

Coutu, Diane, 'Why teams don't work: An interview with J Richard Hackman', *Harvard Business Review*, 2009, https://hbr.org/2009/05/why-teams-dont-work, accessed 28 February 2020.

Cross, Rob, Roeb Rebele and Adam Grant, 'Collaborative overload', *Harvard Business Review*, 2016, https://hbr.org/2016/01/collaborative-overload, accessed 28 February 2020.

Deloitte, '2017 Global Human Capital Trends: Rewriting the rules for the digital age', *Deloitte Development LLC*, 2017, https://documents.deloitte.com/insights/HCTrends2017, p2.

Doran, George, 'There's a S.M.A.R.T. way to write management's goals and objectives', *Management Review*, 70 (11), 1981, p35–36.

Duhigg, Charles, 'What Google learned from its quest to build the perfect team', *New York Times*, 2016, www.nytimes.com/2016/02/28/magazine/what-google-learned-from-its-quest-to-build-the-perfect-team.html, accessed 28 February 2020.

Duhigg, Charles, *The Power of Habit: Why we do what we do, and how to change*, 2012, Random House, London.

Edmondson, Amy, *Teaming: How organizations learn, innovate, and compete in the knowledge economy*, 2010, Jossey-Bass, Hoboken, NJ.

Gawande, Atul, *The Checklist Manifesto*, 2011, Profile Books, London.

Goldhill, David, 'There is someone alive today who will live to 1000 years old: Why are we living longer than ever?', *The Independent*, 2018, www.independent. co.uk/news/long_reads/live-longer-longevity-stem-cells-ageing-a8332701.html, accessed 23 March 2020.

Gottman, John, *The Seven Principles for Making Marriage Work*, 1999, Harmony Books, London.

Gray, Justin, 'The single most powerful question to ask in an interview', *Inc.com*, 2017, www.inc.com/justin-gray/the-single-most-powerful-question-to-ask-in-an-int.html, accessed 28 February 2020.

Kerr, James, *Legacy: What the All Blacks can teach us about the business of life*, 2013, Constable & Robinson Ltd, London.

Leipzig, Adam, 'How to know your life purpose in 5 minutes', *TEDx Talks*, 2013, www.youtube.com/watch?v=vVsXO9brK7M, accessed 28 February 2020.

Lencioni, Patrick, *The Five Dysfunctions of a Team: A leadership fable*, 2002, Jossey-Bass, Hoboken, NJ.

Lencioni, Patrick, *The Ideal Team Player: How to recognize and cultivate the three essential virtues*, 2016, Jossey-Bass, Hoboken, NJ.

Lencioni, Patrick, *The Truth About Employee Engagement: A fable about addressing the three root causes of job misery*, 2007, Jossey-Bass, Hoboken, NJ.

Lewis, Russell, *Company Commander*, 2013, Virgin Books, London.

McChrystal, Stanley, Tantum Collins, David Silverman and Chris Fussell, *Team of Teams: New rules of engagement for a complex world*, 2015, Penguin, London.

Moussa, Mario, Madeline Boyer and Derek Newberry, *Committed Teams: Three steps to inspiring passion and performance*, 2016, John Wiley & Sons, New York.

NASA Video, 'President Kennedy's speech at Rice University', 2013, www.youtube.com/watch?v=WZyRbnpGyzQ, accessed 28 February 2020.

NPR Author Interviews, 'Atul Gawande's "Checklist" for surgery success', 2010, www.npr.org/templates/story/story.php?storyId=122226184, accessed 28 February 2020.

Pentland, Alex 'Sandy', 'The new science of building great teams', *Harvard Business Review*, 2012, https://hbr.org/2012/04/the-new-science-of-building-great-teams, accessed 28 February 2020.

Peters, Steve, *The Chimp Paradox: The mind management programme to help you achieve success, confidence and happiness*, 2012, Vermilion, London.

Rod, Anne and Marita Fridjhon, *Creating Intelligent Teams*, 2016, KR Publishing, Braynstown, South Africa.

Roghanizad, M Mahdi and Vanessa K Bohns, 'Ask in person: You're less persuasive than you think over email', *Journal of Experimental Social Psychology*, 69, 2017, p223–226.

Rozovsky, Julia, 'The five keys to a successful Google team', *re:Work*, 2015, https://rework.withgoogle.com/blog/five-keys-to-a-successful-google-team, accessed 28 February 2020.

Sinek, Simon, *Start with Why: How create leaders inspire everyone to take action*, 2009, Penguin, London.

Tech Insider, 'How Google builds the perfect team', 2016, www.youtube.com/watch?v=v2PaZ8Nl2T4, accessed 28 February 2020.

TED Radio Hour, 'The meaning of work', 2015, www.npr.org/programs/ted-radio-hour/443411154/the-meaning-of-work, accessed 28 February 2020.

Tuckman, Bruce, 'Developmental sequence in small groups', *Psychological Bulletin*, 63 (6), 1965, 384–99.

'TV Home: Cowshed conversion in Somerset', *Grand Designs Magazine*, no date, www.granddesignsmagazine.com/grand-designs-houses/22-tv-home-cowshed-conversion-in-somerset, accessed 28 February 2020.

Various, *HBR's 10 Must Reads – On Collaboration*, 2013, Harvard Business Review Press, Brighton, MA.

Various, *HBR's 10 Must Reads – On Teams*, 2013, Harvard Business Review Press, Brighton, MA.

Wiseman, Liz, *Multipliers: How the best leaders make everyone smarter*, 2010, Harper Business, New York.

Woolley, Anita and Thomas Malone, 'Defend your research: What makes a team smarter? More women', *Harvard Business Review*, 2011, https://hbr.org/2011/06/defend-your-research-what-makes-a-team-smarter-more-women, accessed 28 February 2020.

Wrzesniewski, Amy and Jane Dutton, 'Crafting a job: Revisioning employees as active crafters of their work', *Academy of Management Review*, 26 (2), 2001, p179–201.

Acknowledgements

Books don't write themselves, and the author is just the nib of the pen that writes them. It would be remiss of me not to thank a number of people who contributed, directly or indirectly, in a large or small way, to the creation of this book.

I would like to thank Lucy McCarraher, Caroline Prodger, Joe Gregory and the team at Rethink Press for all their hard work turning my unpolished manuscript into the book you are reading today.

I feel lucky to have had a long list of influential teachers, bosses, trainers, colleagues, teammates, mentors and leaders throughout my life who deliberately or otherwise gave me the opportunity to learn so many of the lessons in teamwork that form a good proportion of this book. I can't name them all but I would like to thank in particular Ken Hughes, Mike Doyle, Richard Goddard, Bev Mileham, Hazel Jackson, Dennis Stever, Brian Stever, Barbara Kerr, Paddy Nolan, Alex Hewitt, Ben Eustace, Paddy Magill, Guy Baker and the Catalyst Global team, Oliver Sheer, Kingsley Seale, David Bassett, David Powell, Stuart Harris, David Simpson, Rob Lewis and Stuart Rees Jones.

I have experienced the ups and downs of teamwork from various rugby teams I have played in, and my thanks for the lessons and memories go to all my coaches and teammates from Malvern College, SOAS RFC, Henley Hawks, SOAS Old Boys and the Rosslyn Park Hatters. I also learnt invaluable life and leadership lessons from the Malvern College Combined Cadet Force and the University of London Officer Training Corps. Despite ensuring I spent most of my time with them being cold, wet, hungry and tired, I am grateful for the experiences and the friendships that last to this day.

I am blessed with a loving and supportive extended family that have been there for me at various times through thick and thin. I don't need to name them all, but I would in particular like to thank Oupa, Graham, Mum, Dad, Stuart and Tom for everything they have done for me over the years.

Finally, I have my most important team to thank. Thank you to my children, Matilda and Oliver, for being an inspiration to me every day. Most importantly, I am forever grateful to my wife Tanya. You wouldn't be reading this book if it had not been for her unwavering and unconditional love, support and advice.

Thank you to you all.

The Author

 Andy Fieldhouse is a man with a mission: To help people get teamwork right. Andy is passionately interested in helping people and teams answer the fundamental question: 'How can we become a strong, cohesive and successful team, while avoiding the pain that poor teamwork can bring along the way?'

After completing a degree in Asian History at London University's School of Oriental and African Studies, Andy spent the first fourteen years of his career in London, working in the wine trade, financial recruitment, and sports marketing and events, in a variety of roles. This foundation allowed Andy to observe, engage with and manage teams from the inside, figuring out what makes them tick.

By 2008, Andy had decided he wanted to turn his passion for and knowledge of teams and teamwork into a career. He joined Dubai-based training and team building company Biz Group, where he ran the team performance arm of the business. In late 2016, Andy set up The Team Space, using his experience to train and coach teams to help them to get teamwork right. He no longer thinks of his work as a job but instead as a mission or calling to empower teams to reach a state where the experience of working together is a happy and rewarding one and success comes as a result.

Originally from the UK, Andy lives in Dubai with his Australian wife Tanya and their two children. When not working or enjoying time with his family, Andy enjoys the odd round of golf or catching up on reading history books.

To find out more about The Team Space, visit www.theteamspace.com

You may also be interested in www.theteamspace.com/blog

To connect with Andy, please visit www.linkedin.com/in/andrewfieldhouse1

Printed in Great Britain
by Amazon